Putty Medals
and Heroes

The History of Selsey Fire Brigade
1909 – 1939

The Selsey Society
(Local History Group)

© The Selsey Society 2008
Putty Medals and Heroes

ISBN : 978-0-9559401-0-1

Published by The Selsey Society
32 St Peter's Crescent
Selsey
Chichester
West Sussex
PO20 0NA

The right of The Selsey Society to be identified as the author of this work has been asserted by them in accordance with the Copyright, Designs and Patents Act 1988.

All rights reserved. No part of this publication may be produced in any form or by any means – graphic, electronic or mechanical including photocopying, recording, taping or information storage and retrieval systems – without the prior permission, in writing, of the publisher.

A CIP catalogue record of this book
can be obtained from the British Library.

LOTTERY FUNDED

Printed and bound by
RPM Print & Design
2-3 Spur Road
Chichester
West Sussex
PO19 8PR

This book is dedicated to all the 'Heroes',
past and present, without whom our
towns and cities would be less safe.

CONTENTS

Foreword by Andy Horner, District Commander, Chichester,
West Sussex Fire Brigade .... *i*

Introduction .... *iii*

1   In the Beginning 1

2   The First Equipment 9

3   Who Pays? 14

4   All about Hydrants 19

5   Keeping the Equipment in Good Order 29

6   Improving the Equipment 36

7   The Fire Brigade in Trouble 50

8   The Brigade Re-forms 62

9   Demands for a New Fire Engine 74

10 Making the Decision 85

11 A New Fire Engine is Finally Acquired 97

12 Payment and Servicing 107

13 Fires and More Fires 126

14 The Fire Brigade Committee 136

15 The Beginning of the End 141

16 Selsey Fire Brigade Fire Captains 146

     and Finally… 155

     Acknowledgements 157

     List of Fires 159

     Index 161

Foreword

As the present District Commander of Chichester, I felt deeply honoured to be asked to write the foreword for this project as I started my career at Selsey as an 18-year-old fireman.

The book gives a great insight of the problems that faced the community of Selsey before they had their own fire engine and the process they had to go through to obtain that appliance in 1933.

Initially, Selsey was covered by Chichester Fire Service until they got their own appliance. The only thing that has changed over the years is that Chichester Fire Brigade supports the Selsey Fire Brigade as Selsey now has modern equipment, attending a variety of calls such as flooding, car accidents, fires, hazardous chemicals and giving Fire Safety advice.

When I first read the book I thought how things have changed, but have they? We now have modern equipment, but the challenges that face the crew are still the same, fire is still dangerous and the crews still have to have the same courage and fortitude to rush into the fire when others are leaving. Councillors still have to balance the books where the finances are concerned. The crews then and now both have the same dedication to serve their community and long may that continue.

Andy Horner

Introduction

In July 1982 the Clerk to Selsey Parish Council, G R G Gimblett, received a letter from the Accountant at the Selsey Branch of Barclays Bank, advising him that their West Bognor Regis Branch was holding two sacks in safe custody marked with the name of A T Cutts and carrying the legend 'old papers of Selsey Parish Council having no intrinsic value'. These sacks had been held since 1956 and the bank was obviously anxious to be rid of them.

BARCLAYS BANK PLC
Selsey Branch
97 High Street, Selsey, Chichester, West Sussex, PO20 0QN
Telephone: Selsey, West Sussex (0243) 602947 and 604132

```
G.R.G.Gimblett Esq.,                      PSK/JS
Clerk to the Council
Selsey Parish Council
55 High Street                            5th July 1982
SELSEY, Chichester
West Sussex


Dear Mr Gimblett,

SELSEY PARISH COUNCIL

We have been advised by our West Bognor Regis Branch that they
are holding two sacks in safe custody marked with the name of
A.T.Cutts and carrying the legend "old papers of Selsey Parish
Council having no intrinsic value". Apparently these have been
held by them since 1956. It may well be that there will be things
contained in these sacks that you require and if you would care to
contact us we would be pleased to make arrangements for you to
collect these items in order that their contents might be
examined.

Yours faithfully,



P.S.KNIGHT
ACCOUNTANT
```

This letter was duly passed to Peter Ogden who 'volunteered' himself and his long-suffering wife, Phyl, to collect the sacks from the Selsey Branch. He took his trusty bike along too, only to discover that the sacks were enormous. Undeterred, Phyl took custody of one sack and Peter rushed off to the Parish Office with the other. He then returned and collected the second sack.

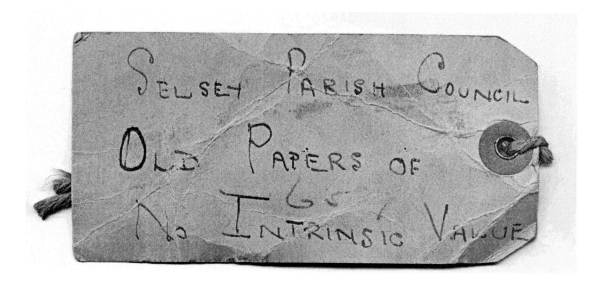

As a self-confessed 'history nut' of many years, he couldn't resist looking at and sorting the contents of the sacks once they had reached his home. The 'old papers' turned out to be the records of Selsey Parish Council, dating back to its foundation in 1894. Amongst them were the Minutes of the Parish Meetings which included information about the formation of the Selsey Fire Brigade.

The idea was born!

The Selsey Society (Local History Group) formed the Selsey Fire Brigade Research Committee consisting of the ubiquitous Peter Ogden along with Peter Rudman, Cynthia Lawson, John Mariner (himself a former retained fireman) and his wife Ruth. The Committee was charged with the responsibility of producing a formal history of the Selsey Fire Brigade from the time of its inception in 1909 to 1939, when the authority was transferred to Chichester Rural District Council. This book is the result.

1 – In the Beginning

Many things can happen in a parish, none more spectacular or dangerous than a fire, yet despite the fact that the Parish Council had powers to provide fire equipment, it took fourteen years for the subject to be raised within their deliberations.

From the beginning the Church had a duty to care for the needy and they developed this role further when the civil forms of relief were being tainted by mismanagement and corruption. Churchwardens were the Overseers by reason of their office and were the valuers, tax collectors and rate assessors. This initiative became the 'Vestry' and was presided over by the vicar. With the churchwardens and a few of the village worthies, the Vestry ruled the roost and was the *de facto* Parish Council.

The Local Government Act 1894 completely changed the administration of the country. Power passed from the unelected Vestries to the newly-formed and elected Parish Councils and this happened in Selsey in December of that year.

In the beginning the Selsey Parish Council had to find its feet and had many things to do in its attempt to introduce democracy in the rural areas. It was not until October 1908 that the subject of a fire engine was raised. Was this because there were no fires, or so few that any such fires were of little consequence? This one, reported in the 'Observer and West Sussex Recorder' on 22nd August 1900, is an example:

A Selsey Sensation

Selsey has broken the record of a thousand years and indulged in a sensation.

On Saturday night, or rather very early indeed on Sunday morning, at ten minutes to one o'clock to be precise, a mysterious fire broke out on the bathing ranche at the corner of the New-road.[1]

The fire did not last long but it worked well and did a deal of damage for its size. In about ten minutes, Fisher's bathing hut, The Pierrot party's stage and Captain Pelham's bathing tent and all that therein was, were reduced to cinders and matters of history.

---

[1] Now Hillfield Road.

How the fire originated nobody seems to know. A good deal of abuse was at first hurled at the stove in Fisher's bathing hut. At one time there was even talk of arresting its charred remains on suspicion. Mr Fisher, however, stated that he put the stove out at half-past five on the previous afternoon, so that the stove is effectually absolved from all blame. Meantime Selsey has turned its mighty brain towards the discovery how the fire began. No solution to the problem has yet been found but it is said that five hundred people, including the local constable, who owing to press of business, did not reach the scene of the fire until Sunday, have several thousand clues to work on.

Anyhow the little history of the fire is quite romantic.

The last tired mother had dragged the last fractious child home to bed, the last pater had smoked his last cigar upon the beach and the last Saturday night lover had breathed a last passionate good-night to his beloved. Silence, save for the eternal murmur of the sea settled down upon Selsey, and the little town, all ignorant of the tragedy to come, sank into slumber.

One soul alone remained with sleepless eyelids, that was Frank the barman of the new Marine Hotel. Why he remained awake is a mystery too. Some say that love was the secret cause, others declare that a heavy supper off Chichester pie was the true reason. Anyhow, Frank, who refuses to answer questions on the matter remained awake upon his little white couch and gazed at the stars through his open window.

Just before one o'clock the unwonted smell of smoke cannoned his nostrils. With all the agility of a fine young barman in good condition, Frank jumped out of bed and ran to the window. He saw a tongue of flame doing a pas de seul upon the top of Fisher's bathing hut.

He was rushing from the room when he remembered his "be-nighted" condition, he donned his every-day garments with modesty and haste and tore out to the rescue. With great presence of mind he cut the ropes of Pelham's tent, meaning to save the piano, but the tent was so intensely hot that the moment the ropes were cut the tent burst into a mass of flame. Frank states that he heard the piano trying nobly to play "God Save the Queen" with its last dying note.

Fisher's hut was by now lapped in flame. Frank looked despairingly at the sea: there was plenty of water but no means of putting out the fire, he thought of laying on the beer from the hotel cellars but time was too short to permit of this, so he contented himself in saving Capt. Pelham's second bathing tent. In fact, but for the promptitude of Frank Elliott, the fire would have been far worse. Loud popped the ginger beer bottles stored in Fisher's tent as the fire reached them. The Coastguards sleeping faithful at their (bed) posts heard that and started up. Visions of a French invasion floated before their frightened eyes. They reached for their cutlass and scampered out resolved to sell their lives as dearly as they could. It is said that they were immensely relieved when they found that heroic self-sacrifice was not necessary. With a final burst of flames the fire gave its dying kick and went out. The coastguards powerless to do anything stood by with the greatest gallantry and watched it. Then the sun came up over the Bill and the coast-guards went back to bed and Capt. Pelham came down to look at the damage. It was considerable. Mr Fisher must have lost a good deal, but Capt. Pelham lost heavily. Besides the piano a new and expensive one and the stage he lost the gear and sails of two or three boats and a number of bathing costumes and towels. Many visitors too had their things destroyed. The scene after the fire was most remarkable and experts say they have seldom seen anything so extraordinary. The ground was swept clean. Absolutely nothing remained but bits of charred wood, the iron frame of piano, a few of its strings, and some ginger beer bottles and tea cups which had been fused together owing to the great heat. The stove which was at first thought had caused the fire seemed the least damaged of all.

In spite of the loss of the piano the usual sacred concert was held on Sunday night thanks to Capt. Pelham's enterprise and the kindness of a gentleman, who lent an instrument.

The latest reports from Selsey state that visitors are still wandering over the scene of the fire with their hands pressed to their brows, thinking deeply. Perhaps in a year or so when they have had time to think properly they may find out how that fire was caused. That is of course if someone else does not find out sooner, which is quite probable.

The writer of this lengthy report used it mainly as an opportunity to poke fun at Selsey, and there is no suggestion that fire fighting equipment should have been available…so what happened to ignite the sudden concern several years later?

Although the Selsey Fire Station of today is fully equipped with up-to-date fire-fighting apparatus, there was a time when the only equipment consisted of a hose and standpipe which had to be pushed to the scene of the fire on a handcart.

If the fire seemed to be too big for the local volunteers to deal with, then a call for help would be sent to Chichester, and, within what seemed to be a surprisingly short time, the fire-engine, drawn by two lathered horses, would dash to the blaze.

'Fighting the Flames'

The Chichester Brigade was formed about 1872, and consisted of a hand cart laden with leather hose and some very long, branch pipes. Then, in 1906, Chichester became 'the proud owner of a horse drawn steam fire engine and every turn out became an event of great interest and excitement to the worthy citizens, the sight of the galloping horses drawing a smoking, steaming monster through the streets of the city providing a heart stirring spectacle'. It is this 'monster' which attended the first recorded fires in Selsey, such as this rick fire at Common Farm (now North Common Farm) reported in the 'Observer and West Sussex Recorder', 1st September 1909:

Struck by Lightning – Rick Fired at Selsey

During the short, sharp storm which passed over the district on Wednesday afternoon, a corn rick, belonging to Mr James Clayton, of Common Farm, Selsey, was struck by lightning, a hole being driven right through, the middle and the interior becoming ignited. News was at once sent to Chichester, and the fire bell attracted a large crowd to Eastgate Square to witness the departure of the engine. Rain was falling heavily, and a high wind prevented the sound of the bell travelling in but one direction. However, Captain Budden, with firemen Hopkins and Welcome were quickly on the scene, and the engine was soon on its way to Selsey. Second Officer Holt, who, by the way, had himself been stranded owing to the effect of the lightning on his motor car, put in an appearance immediately afterwards, and overtook the engine at the "Four Chestnuts", where, throwing his bicycle by the roadside, he scrambled on to the engine as it galloped round the bend on the way to Hunston. Another fireman was picked up on the road, so that the engine arrived at Selsey under the hour with five men, which is ample to enable the steamer to get to work.

North Common Farm as it is today

Other firemen arrived later, and, thanks to the efforts of the Brigade, more than half the rick was saved. When the Brigade arrived, little had been done to check the fire, which, so far was confined to the interior of the rick. The firemen at once directed operations by digging out the burning portion. The flames had not yet broken out through the walls of the rick, so men got on to the top and threw a large portion of the unburnt straw from the rick, damping out the flames which came through as they neared the interior. Fortunately, plenty of water was available from a pond close by, and in a short time, the whole of the damaged portion was dug out, and more than half the rick saved.

Little, of course could be done prior to the arrival of the Brigade, for the nature of the fire was such as rendered it quite impossible to deal with it with water barrels—the only available paraphernalia at the time. A good deal of ridicule was expressed by a critical crowd who assembled at Eastgate to witness the departure of the Brigade, and it is no thanks to them that the Brigade got away as quickly as it did. Councillor Aylmore (Chairman of the Fire Brigade Committee) was among the first at the engine house, and rendered appreciable assistance.

In summary, in 1893 the Vestry was legally required to provide a Fire Service and by 1894 the new Parish Council had the necessary powers to obtain, either by acquiring, purchasing or borrowing, a fire engine and the equipment to go with it. It could also claim expenses for maintenance and storage and could fund the provision of firemen. The fact that the Chichester Brigade galloped down to Selsey, apparently without charge, suggests that the Vestry had made an arrangement under the Town Police Clauses Act 1847.

It was eventually realised that waiting for the horse-drawn fire engine to arrive from Chichester was not the most effective way to deal with local fires. However, certain facilities had to be in place before an effective Fire Brigade could be formed, most notably an efficient supply of mains water.

At the end of 1906 a debate was in full flow as to who should have the right to supply Selsey with water. The right to supply water lay with the City Council under the Chichester Corporation Water Act 1897 but for reasons of finance no steps had been taken to exercise this right. The idea of potential power being removed from them disturbed the City Fathers and they argued about the best way forward.

In January 1907, the Parish Clerk reported that a Bill had been applied for to supply Selsey (and elsewhere) with water and gas. The Bill included powers to lay mains and had sections relating to the cost of supply. This Bill also aimed to repeal the Water Act already in place. The councillors debated this hotly, wondering whether to oppose the plans, and called for an engineer's report. The proposed Bill covered the supply of water not only to Selsey but also to the surrounding parishes of Sidlesham, Birdham, Earnley, East and West Wittering, Hunston and North Mundham.

The Parish Council then received a letter from Messrs Wyatts acting as agents for Selsey-on-Sea Limited. According to the West Sussex Gazette of the time, the stated aim of this company was to 'acquire certain lands and hereditaments known as the Selsey Estates, to develop and turn to account any of the company's property by building, cultivating, letting on building lease or agreement, or otherwise, and to construct or acquire railways, steamers, motors, tramways, baths, golf courses, sea defences, &c.' In short, Selsey-on-Sea Limited wanted to own and run Selsey and turn it into a 'seaside resort'. The letter asked the Parish Council to pass a resolution in support of a scheme by the said company and oppose the Bill before Parliament. However, it was decided that in the absence of any information about the scheme, their charges, and so on, the Council could not pass any resolution on the matter.

According to a report in the 'West Sussex Gazette' on 14th March 1907:

> *It would seem that Selsey and Chichester are likely to come to some sort of terms for a supply of water from the city mains, at least, that is the impression to be gathered from what was said by Mr W H B Fletcher JP at the Westhampnett Council meeting on Friday. It appears that the Council had been approached, in reference to Selsey-on-Sea Ltd with a view to their considering any alternative scheme for the supply of water to Selsey. Having regard to the attitude they took up with reference to the Selsey Water Bill, the Council would not undertake to consider any alternative scheme. Mr Fletcher intimated that since the promoters of the Bill first set to work, a change in the position had arisen which might result in Selsey getting its water supply at very short notice. 'I believe they are trying to come to an arrangement with certain authorities for a supply of water', said Mr Fletcher. He added that he had received an intimation that the promoters would need to acquire certain land of his at Mundham, in regard to which negotiations had passed.*

Owing to the intransigent attitude of the Corporation, efforts had been made to locate a local supply of water, but even a 100 foot-deep borehole had failed to meet the required supply.

In 1907 the Selsey Water Company presented a Bill before Parliament to supply Selsey with water and on the 25th July 1907 the Selsey Bill passed into law. With commendable speed, the company was formed and all the preparations completed, so that the following report could be made on the 24th June 1908:

> *The work of connecting the water supply from Chichester to Selsey commenced on Thursday last; the village in consequence will shortly boast a constant source at high pressure.*

On 19th December 1908 the Waterworks in Cross Road (now School Lane) was opened and reported in the 'Chichester Observer' as follows:

> *Water, water, everywhere. Roads ankle deep in mud and water, rain falling in miserable drizzle and a breeze coming from the sea and the enveloping mist sent a chill to the very marrow. Such were the conditions which prevailed at Selsey on Saturday when the Mayor of Chichester Alderman Holt officially opened the Selsey Water Works. After the opening the Company retired to the Station Hotel for refreshments.*

Seven and a half miles of five inch cast iron pipes were laid and a water tower was planned as a reserve. A newspaper report stated that:

> *The height of the Chichester water towers is sufficient to ensure a good pressure for the delivery of the Selsey supply. Some 20 hydrants have so far been fixed along the route of the main, with approval of the Corporation Surveyor, and 13 more have to be provided as found necessary. These hydrants will of course, be invaluable in case of an outbreak of fire, in which emergency the Company have undertaken to supply the water free of charge. The capacity of the mains is said to be no less than 120,000 gallons a day… The Chichester Corporation, it is understood, are under an obligation to supply water continuously at adequate pressure.*

There were also problems of sanitation and the Parish Council minutes are full of complaints about obnoxious smells emerging from various parts of the village. Sanitation, therefore, would be an additional reason why it was important to have new water mains installed.

The Chichester Corporation now supplied the water to the Selsey Water Company and over the years there was a continuous battle over its cost.

2 – The First Equipment

Residents with buckets are replaced by a hose cart

At long last, 14 years after the establishment of the Parish Council, we find a minute of a meeting dated 13th October 1908:

> *Fire Appliances. The question of providing a fire engine was mentioned and the matter was left to the General Purposes Committee.*

It was nine months before the Committee reported as follows:

> *Your Committee has under consideration the question of the supply of Fire Extinguishing appliances for the Parish and it is recommended that the Council should purchase fire hose and fittings.*
>
> *(Signed) E G Arnell*

The report was discussed and it was proposed by S Dewey, seconded by W E G Arnell and resolved that the last clause relating to the provision of Fire Extinguishing appliances be referred back to the Committee for further consideration and the matter placed on the Agenda for discussion at the next meeting. At this next meeting, in October 1909, it was minuted:

> *Fire Extinguishing Appliances. Your Committee have very fully considered the question of providing fire extinguishing appliances in the parish and have had an interview with W A J Cutler, ex-Captain of the Chichester Fire Brigade who has kindly given his assistance.*

Mr Cutler explained that, in his opinion, the necessary appliances would cost about £15, made up as follows:

	£	s	d
2 lengths of hose (80 feet)	10	0	0
Stand post	2	16	0
Turn Key		7	6
Wrenches		10	0
Nozzle	1	0	0
Box for same		10	0
Total	£15	3	6

A formal request for information was made to Messrs Shand Mason & Co. and they advised that a hose cart and all necessary gear for dealing with a fire in a district where hydrants were installed would cost £50.

While all this discussion was taking place there was another fire on Tuesday 30th November 1909, this time at Hilton's Farm (also known as Foot's Farm, situated on the corner of West Street, approximately where the Riviera is today), and it was reported in two local newspapers, the 'West Sussex Gazette' on 2nd December 1909 and also the 'Chichester Observer'. Fortunately the damage to the property was covered by insurance.

The following report is taken from the Chichester Observer of 8th December 1909:

Fire at Selsey
Farm Buildings and Bathing Machines Destroyed
Chichester Brigade's Smart Turn Out

A fire, which resulted in the destruction of £400 worth of property, occurred at Hilton's Farm,[2] Selsey, on Tuesday evening last, and caused a good deal of excitement in the village, a large crowd assembling at the scene of the out-break.

Hilton's Farm

---
[2] Mrs Hilton was 'a London lady'.

The fire was discovered by Mr Titchenor, and the occupier of the buildings, Mr. Percy Legg, was at once informed, and a telephonic communication sent to Chichester [at about 9pm] summoning the aid of the Fire Brigade.

Within ten minutes after the message was received the Brigade, to the number of seventeen men, including Captain Budden and Second Officer Holt, with the steamer, was on their way to Selsey. A large crowd had assembled at Eastgate, attracted by the clanging of the fire bell,[3] and as the Brigade dashed away, signified their appreciation of the smart turn out by a cheer. Councillors Aylmore, Garland, and Bottrill, were among the first to arrive at the Fire Station, and rendered what assistance they could.

Although efforts had been made locally to extinguish the flames by throwing buckets of water over the burning building, by the time the Brigade had reached Selsey, the fire had a good hold on the buildings, from the thatched roof of which flames shot out high in the air. Within, a dozen bathing machines belonging to Mr Percy Wren, of Chichester, were well ablaze, while the contents of the cart and corn sheds and stables were also too much damaged to necessitate the attention of the Brigade, who, finding it impossible to save the buildings, set to work to prevent the fire from spreading to the cottages adjoining, and in this they were successful.

Fortunately, no live stock was lost, but a quantity of barley, potatoes, etc, was completely destroyed.

There was, happily, thanks to the new supply at Selsey, plenty of water with which the Brigade could play upon the flames, and two jets were brought into operation. The Brigade worked strenuously, and were greatly assisted by several willing local helpers. They remained upon the scene until about three o'clock, when the condition of the buildings justified them in leaving, and they reached Chichester about four o'clock in the morning.

Credit is due to the many residents, who did all in their power to check the flames prior to the arrival of the brigade from Chichester, but with only buckets at their command, their efforts were of little avail.

It was this fire at Hilton's Farm that prompted the purchase of fire fighting equipment, as a Special Meeting of the Selsey Parish Council was held a week later, on 7th December, to consider the question of providing fire extinguishing appliances for the Parish. It was finally proposed by W Fogden, seconded by W Meades and unanimously resolved:

---

[3] Electric bells weren't installed in the Firemen's houses until 1910.

That the Clerk be instructed to purchase from Messrs Shand Mason & Co the necessary appliances named by them in their letter of the 10th November 1909 in accordance with their specification and estimate contained in such letter, as follows:-

	£	s	d
Metropolitan Brigade pattern hand hose and implement cart complete and lettered S.P.C. as per specification	14.	0.	0
Lamps	2.	0.	0
4. 100 feet lengths and 250 feet lengths of Hose as per Specification aforesaid	14.	10.	0
2 Branch pipes	1.	5.	0
2 Wrenches		5.	0
Stand Pipe	3.	10.	0
Hand pump complete	1.	17.	0
Helmets	2.	8.	0
Belts, axes etc	3.	0.	0
Total	£42.	15.	0

The Clerk was also instructed to purchase a T-key (turnkey) at 12s.6d and sufficient hydrant indicating plates. The question of detail was left in the hands of the General Purposes Committee. This was one of the first references to hydrants in the Parish Council's records and the issue was never far away.

At a meeting on 11th January 1910, the Clerk, in reply to a question by W Fogden, read correspondence relative to the purchase of fire extinguishing appliances from which it was shown that the goods were ordered on 8th December and that the Clerk had also been in communication with Mr Cutler, the Chichester Fire Brigade and the Selsey Water Company. Mr Cutler had replied that it would give him pleasure to do anything that might be beneficial to the well-being of the inhabitants of the village. The Chichester Fire Brigade had sent patterns of hydraulic top and hose coupling which had been forwarded to Shand Mason & Co. and four firemen's helmets were also ordered.

On 20th April 1910 the bill from Shand Mason, amounting to £43.18s.0d, was received and the Chairman asked to confer with W Cutler on the matter with a view to getting everything in readiness in case of fire.

3 – Who Pays?

He who pays the piper calls the tune (but not, apparently, in Selsey).

It was June 1910 when the trouble started. A letter from Chas. M C Wakely of The Manor, Selsey, to The Local Government Board Office in Whitehall, London, dated 2nd June 1910, stated:

Dear Sir

Am extremely sorry to trouble you, but there is a great grievance being caused in this Parish by the Rate-payers being called upon to pay a Rate levied by the Parish Council for the payment for Fire Appliances. Their contention is that it is not legal for the Council to enforce this payment which is on the Land as well as Houses, while the Council has never adopted the Lighting and Watching Act of 1833; the contention is, even if the Council had adopted this Act, the charge on Land should be excepted. It seems to me Section 19 subsection 9, is quite clear on this point. Our contention is that this Rate is quite illegal to be charged in with general expenses of the Parish Council and not even shown in the list of expenses in the column on the Rate Book.

Several of the Parish Councillors are with those who are objecting to pay this Rate. I shall esteem it a great favour to hear from you in reference to this important matter and thank you in anticipation.

Faithfully Yours

A copy of this letter was forwarded to the Parish Council of Selsey asking them to 'furnish the observations of the Council on the subject of that letter' to the Local Government Board.

The transfer of powers from the Vestry to the Parish Council brought with it responsibility for the Overseers, who had survived the handover and were still charged with setting and collecting the rates. Having had a demand from the Council to cover the cost of purchase of the fire equipment, they had to collect the amount required. This was set by them based on the valuation they had made on each property. Grumbling about rates was not new and this demand had Mr Wakely leading the charge.

The Clerk to the Selsey Parish Council, Mr Ide, responded to a request for details of the actions taken by the Council leading to the purchase of the fire equipment as follows:

...At the beginning of December a fire broke out in Selsey Main Street.[4] A hydrant was close by but no appliance at hand for obtaining water from it. The Brigade from Chichester was called (which is 8 miles distant) but the premises were gutted. Houses on the opposite side of the road were threatened, and I am informed, only the extreme exertions of the Coastguard and others prevented a very disastrous conflagration...

December 7th, 1909 a special meeting of the Council was held for the purpose of considering the question. 8 of the 11 Councillors were present together with the Chairman (Elected from outside the Council).

The matter was fully gone into and it was unanimously resolved to purchase Fire Extinguishing Appliances to the cost of about £43.

He also reported that the Overseers had been issued with a precept of £40 to meet current expenses of the Council and that the Overseers had inserted this in the Poor Rate Demand Note. He stated that the Council had moved in this matter under the Poor Law Amendment Act 1867, in conjunction with the Local Government Act of 1894, Sec. 6, c.2, as being the most simple and least expensive course, bearing in mind that the expense was for one half year only. If the Lighting and Watching Act 1833 had been adopted Mr Wakely's objection would still have existed.

The Local Government Board responded in true Civil Service fashion:

...The Board have no authority to interfere in this matter...

but then went on to quote various authorities whereby the Council could legally purchase the equipment and levy the rate.

Meanwhile, the topic was under discussion in the local newspapers and on 20th July 1910, the 'Bognor Observer' reported:

Fire Precautions

An old inhabitant of Selsey writes: - "After some 18 months consideration the Selsey Parish Council, urged on by the voice of the people in general and by the trouble to prevent the spreading of fire during a recent outbreak in the High Street, resolved

---

[4] Hilton's Farm - see chapter 2

to purchase lengths of hose and other appliances for immediate use in the event of another outbreak, with the right to use the water from the Selsey Water Company, a course which seemed to meet with general approval. The hose was purchased and arrangements made for its being accessible without delay. But three or four ratepayers, who have land in addition to house and buildings, seemed to consider themselves aggrieved as it would mean a very slight rate (for one half-year only) on their land, and in their wisdom convened a meeting at the Crown Inn on Monday of last week to protest against the same, but who attended or what took place at the meeting has not been made public. Really in these days it is seldom we hear of objections to any action taken to prevent the spread of fire and we await with interest the action of this especially small number of gentlemen who would prefer a fire to spread rather than pay for one half-year rate of $^5/_8$ of a 1d in the £ on a few acres of land.

The following week this reply was published:

In answer to the letter signed "An Old Resident", which appeared in last week's issue, Mr Arthur H Woodman of Selsey, writes:

'Sir, - in his letter headed "Fire Precautions", he (the writer) mentions that a meeting was held at the "Crown" on a certain date. He admits that he neither knows who attended or what transpired at the meeting, and yet he manufactures the following statements:

1. *That the meeting was called to protest against the provision of fire appliances for the village.*
2. *That the farmers and landholders object to any action being taken to prevent the spread of a fire.*
3. *That this 'especially small number of gentlemen' would prefer a fire to spread, rather than pay for one half-year a small rate on a few acres of land.*

In making these assertions, "Old Inhabitant" must not expect the general public to agree with him. The facts, as far as I can ascertain them are as follows: a push cart, small hand pump, four brass helmets, and 500 feet of hose pipe have been procured at the expense of the locality. The water main runs through the main street of the village to the Marine Hotel, with branches down West Street and East Road. Only property, therefore, situated on the three roads mentioned, can hope to receive any protection from the fire appliances purchased. "Old Inhabitant" if he chooses to look round, must see, in many parts of the parish, that there are properties – farmhouses, buildings, cottages, etc. – which cannot receive the slightest protection or benefit from the expenditure. This being so, a meeting was called to consider the matter, when it was decided that the just and fair way of defraying the cost was to divide it proportionately amongst those who had any possible chance of receiving benefit should the need unfortunately arise, and that, on principle, it was unfair to expect those to help pay the piper when they had no possible chance of calling the tune.

Yours faithfully,
Arthur H Woodman[5]
Selsey 24 July 1910

On Friday 15th December 1911, a fire at East Beach that started in 'The Shanty' and spread next door to 'Once Was' would have been well out of reach of the fire hoses, and it appears from the following report in the 'Bognor Observer' on 20th December that the Fire Brigade wasn't even called out:

Mysterious Fires

By some cause unknown, the bungalow, 'The Shanty' situated on East Beach, became ignited just after midnight on Friday, and was burned to the ground. A stiff breeze was blowing at the time, with the result that the neighbouring bungalow to leeward caught fire and was also devastated. The second bungalow was 'Once Was' owned by H B Hemmons, and 'The Shanty' belonged to Mrs Cheffins.[6] Both of the houses, which were disused railway carriages, were insured, as were also the contents. Some consternation was naturally aroused among the residents on the Saturday morning when they were notified of the fact, for, with the exception of a few fisherman, etc, there were none who saw the fire.

In 1912, Mr Hemmons was having trouble claiming on his insurance, as related by this rather unsatisfactory report in the 'Bognor Observer':

A Selsey Fire

Sequel in the King's Bench Division

On Monday before Mr Justice Bucknill and a special jury, the hearing in the King's Bench Division was resumed of the action brought by Mr Hy. B. Hemmons, of Cambridge Park Twickenham, against Messrs. F B Cooper & Co, insurance

---

[5] Mr Woodman owned Hales Farm which was halfway down the High Street, opposite Lewis Road.
[6] Possibly Mrs Chaffens.

> brokers. The action was brought in respect of their alleged failure to renew (upon his instructions) a Lloyd's policy of insurance on his bungalow, 'Once Was', at Selsey, which was destroyed by fire in December 1911, and the defendants denied liability.
>
> The case for plaintiff was that he effected a policy for £250 in January, 1911, for a year and subsequently expressed his desire to have the policy renewed, to which end he wrote to the defendants and also 'phoned. The renewal was not carried out, and after the old policy ran out the bungalow was destroyed by fire. It was stated that the defendants denied receiving 'phone instructions.
>
> The defence was that the whole case depended on the 'phone communication, and both Mr Cooper and Mr Garrett (the defendants) as well as the office boy, did not have any conversation, and in cross-examination Mr Cooper admitted that he was liable if the evidence re the 'phone conversation were true.
>
> The hearing was adjourned.

Unfortunately there appears to be neither a record of the start of the action brought by Mr Hemmons, nor a report on what happened after this hearing.

This fire demonstrated Selsey's need for a more readily-available water supply to go with the new fire-fighting equipment and fire hydrants should have resolved this issue.

4 – All about Hydrants

Hydrant – an apparatus for drawing water directly from a main, consisting of a pipe with one or more nozzles, or with a spout or the like.[7]

The following chapter must form an integral part of any Fire Brigade history – after all, where would the Fire Brigade be without access to water?

The reference to 33 hydrants at the end of chapter 1 is somewhat puzzling in the light of the story of hydrants which is recounted below.

On 22nd October 1912, Mr Cutler wrote to the Parish Clerk as follows:

> *Some nearly three years ago I consented to act as Captain of the Fire Brigade for the village but I find my time now fully occupied and also advancing in years, really must ask your Council's indulgence to remove my name and responsibility from same, but representing the Water Company, I have no doubt and hope to render any service if called upon, but take the opportunity to say that the village is very short and scantily supplied with fire hydrants and should a serious fire occur, there will cause a great comment at some future date.*

His letter was read out at the Parish Council's meeting on 25th February 1913. Mr Cutler's resignation was accepted with regret and he was thanked for the trouble he had taken during his time as Captain.

As a result, the Council requested from the Rural District Council a plan showing the number and position of hydrants in order to ascertain whether the Water Company had carried out their agreement to provide and maintain fifteen hydrants in Selsey. They also considered the advisability of obtaining plates showing the position of the hydrants and the question of storage for the equipment.

On 1st May 1913 a list of hydrants had been supplied as follows:

---

[7] Oxford English Dictionary

No of hydrant	Situation of Hydrant
1.	On the main road at Norton, opposite Compton's Barn.
2.	On the main road opposite the entrance to Selsey Rectory.
3.	On the main road opposite the United Methodist Chapel.
4.	On the main road opposite the Crown Inn.
5.	In East Street, Selsey, opposite the residence of Mr H A Smith (No 48).
6.	In East Street opposite the "Fisherman's Joy Inn".

(all the above to be inserted in the line of main from Chichester to Selsey)

The following sites were selected for insertion of hydrants on the contributory mains when laid:

7.	Opposite the Village Green in East Street.
8.	Opposite the Albion Inn in East Street.
9.	At Fish Shop's Road End.(Coast Guards Lane)
10.	Opposite the Blacksmith's shop in the occupation of Mr C Wingham at the junction of West Street.
11.	Opposite the residence of Mr A J Cutler in New Road.
12.	Opposite the residence of Mr Bransby Williams in New Road.
13.	Opposite the Marine Hotel in New Road.
14.	Opposite the Blacksmith's shop in West Street.
15.	Opposite the residence of Mr J Mitchell in West Street.

On receipt of the list the Council requested Mr Cutler, who was a builder, to bring the hydrants up to road level, to be kept clear and to be given notice when this was done. The work was apparently completed within the week. Mr Cutler also provided a quotation for the provision and fixing of fire hydrant signs at six shillings each.

A new list of hydrants was drawn up three years later which indicates that the number had increased considerably from the previous list of 1913, though it was not up to the number of 33 referred to in the 1908 newspaper report.

Provision of Fire Hydrants in the Parish of Selsey

	Street	Position	Distance from wall etc.
1.	High Street	Opposite Rectory Gate	35' 6" from gate
2.	High Street	Opposite United Methodist Chapel	3' 6" from garden wall of house next to Godels
3.	High Street	Opposite Crown Inn	3' from sign post
4.	High Street	Facing West Street	12' from Wingham's wall
5.	Hillfield Road	Opposite Hillinglea close to lamp post	11' 6" from wall
6.	Hillfield Road	Opposite Somerleigh	18' 3" from gate
7.	Hillfield Road	Opposite Marine Hotel	18' 6" from gate
8.	West Street	Opposite Male's Forge	9' from wall
9.	West Street	Opposite end of Clayton Road	17' from Clayton's wall
10.	West Street	Opposite Danner Coast Guard Street	3' from wall
11.	East Road	Opposite Banff House	12' from wall
12.	Lower East Street	Opposite 2 Cotlands nr Green	19' 6" from wall
13.	Albion Road	Opposite telephone post below Albion Inn	15' 6" from pole
14.	Coast Guard Lane Fishing Beach	Opposite C G Houses gate	11' 6" from garden fence
15.	Lewis Road	Opposite Ralda	23' from Ralda
16.	North Road	Opposite Baroona	9' from gate
17.	Manor Road	Opposite Fisherman's Joy	14' 6" from wall
18.	Manor Road	Opposite Selsey Hotel	50' from garden fence
19.	Station Road	Opposite builders' yard gate (late H J Hart)	47' from gate
20.	Grafton Road	Opposite Emlyn	50' from fence
21.	Vincent Road	Opposite Tetsworth House	
22.	Norton Priory	Opposite Denmans Gate	
23.	Norton (main road) near Council Cottages		Same side of the road 50' towards Coffins House

24.	East Beach	Back gate of Dunrobin	About 4' towards Park
25.	East Beach	Telephone kiosk	4' from box
26.	East Beach	Corner of Serena	Corner nearest Wi-Wurry

The Rural District Council had already been requested not to tar over the hydrant cover plates when tar spraying, to ensure that the plates were left uncovered.

Now that the locations of the hydrants were known, it was discovered that three or four were not available for use and Mr Cutler was asked to ensure that all the hydrants in the Parish were made and kept clear. The Parish Council would then like to inspect them. In spite of this request being made in October 1913, the Clerk reported in the following January that no reply had been received. However, it appears that the hydrants had been properly inspected and by the following July were in a satisfactory condition.

***

Several years later, in 1920, it was reported that the fire equipment had been tested and that new equipment was required. At the same time it was pointed out that some properties in the village were too far from hydrants for a hose to reach them, so it was decided that a letter should be sent to the owners of these properties stating this and that the following letter should be sent to all the owners in Seal and Clayton Roads:

Dear Sir,

At a meeting of the Selsey Parish Council on the 12th inst. [i.e. 12th October 1920] *I was instructed to inform you that the Council have 500ft. of fire hose which they are having placed in a serviceable condition. As your property is some distance from the nearest hydrant, the fire-extinguishing appliance belonging to the Council would be useless in the event of an outbreak of a fire upon your premises. They would therefore suggest that you took such steps as to secure the insertion of a hydrant within reasonable distance of your premises.*

I am, Sir,
Yours faithfully,
S. Dewey, Clerk

It appears that although the above letter was drawn up in 1920, it was not sent out. It was nearly two years later, in July 1922, that the Committee instructed the Clerk to send it out as soon as the fire equipment was in a satisfactory condition.

In the Fire Committee's report of October 1922 the following is included:

> *We have made an investigation of Water Hydrants and although we were furnished with a list of about 8 or 9 we have discovered 17 in all. A plan or list of these has been made and measurements taken from the nearest wall, building or fence and we suggest the necessity of immediately putting F H indicators, in such positions that the location of hydrants can be immediately ascertained and we ask for your authority to put this work in hand.*

> *We found that four of the hydrants were covered either by road material or grass and on application to the surveyor three have been brought into view but we are advised that we must put indicators where needed or this will be done by the District Council and the cost charged to us which we venture to suggest will be higher than if the work is done by local men. A fourth hydrant situated in a private (though important) road remains undiscovered – we shall either have to get the landlord of property nearest to do this work or have it done at Parish Council expense, which will only be a very small matter. We have opened and inspected one hydrant and found the connecting screw very rusty, and we presume all are in the same condition. It is necessary that all hydrants should be inspected without delay and the screws and valves properly cleaned and lubricated. This inspection should be done periodically by the Firemen so that quick connection may be ensured when required.*

Fire hydrant indicator plates were purchased as suggested and it was reported that:

> *Hydrant indicator plates have arrived from the makers and will shortly be fixed to their respective positions. Special thanks should be accorded to PC Pope for his valuable assistance in testing hydrants and in other ways giving us help.*

Three months later the committee also reported:

> *Every hydrant in the village has been tested and the pressure of water is satisfactory except for high buildings such as the Marine Hotel. The Water Company have been asked to make arrangements with the Chichester Works to have increased pressure available when required.*

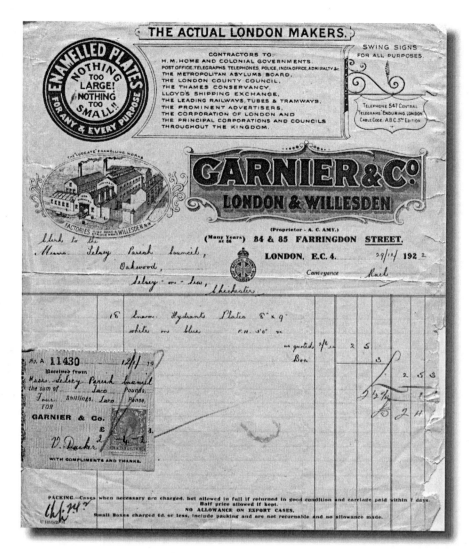

Invoice for Hydrant Plates

It is strange that in 1922 the Brigade had lost sight of the fire hydrants despite the fact that, in 1913 and again in 1916, every hydrant had been located. In 1913 there were 16 and in 1916 there were 26, yet now only 17 could be found.

In October 1931 a list giving the location of 31 hydrants was provided by the Westhampnett Rural District Council to Selsey Parish Council but the accompanying letter from Mr Rasell, Clerk to the Council, stated that the Selsey Water Company had been asked to produce a plan showing the position of the mains supplying the existing hydrants. This plan was required to enable the Rural District Council to insert the position of the additional hydrants.

Despite several requests, this plan was not forthcoming, so Mr Vince, Clerk to the Parish Council, was asked to bring the matter up at the next Parish Council meeting and informed that, once the information had been received '...the Rural District Council will be prepared to take all necessary steps to give effect thereto'.

FIRE HYDRANTS IN THE PARISH OF SELSEY

1	35' 6"	From Rectory Gate	High Street
2	3' 6"	.. Garden wall of house next to Shop (Godels)	.. ..
3	3' 0"	.. Sign post outside of "Crown Inn"	.. ..
4	12' 0"	.. Wall, facing West Street	.. ..
5	11' 6"	.. Wall opposite "Hillingly"	Hillfield Road
6	18' 2"	.. .. .. "Somerleigh"	.. ..
7	18' 6"	.. Marine Hotel Gate	.. ..
8	28' 0"	.. Tetsworth House Fence	Vincent Road
9	3' 0"	.. Coastguard Station Garden Wall	West Street
10	17' 6"	.. Claytons Wall (End of Clayton Rd)	.. ..
11	8' 6"	.. Opposite Males Forge	.. ..
12	33' 0"	.. "Byrerly"	Coxes Road
13	29' 0"	.. "Glengarrie" (top of -- --)	Grafton Road
14	34' 0"	From Garden Wall of "Staffa"	.. ..
15	3' 0"	.. Fence of "Wynshaven"	Lewes Road
16	12' 0"	.. Wall opposite Banff House	East Road
17	19' 6"	.. Cotlands Wall	Lower East Road
18	15' 6"	.. Telephone post, below Albion Inn	Albion Road
19	11' 6"	.. Fence of old Coast Guard Stn. Garden.	Coast Guard Lane
20	9' 0"	Opposite "Welback", below St. Albans	Fishing Beach Bungalows
21	14' 6"	From "Fisherman's Joy Inn" Wall	Manor Road
22	50' 0"	.. Garden Fence of The Selsey Hotel	.. ..
23	47' 0"	.. Fence of Building Yard (Late Hart's)	Station Road
24	9' 0"	.. "Baroona", Garden Wall	North Road
25	30' 6"	.. "Innerleithen" (temporary)	Bonnar Road
26	28' 0"	.. Fence of Bill House, North side of gate	Upper Grafton Road
27	4' 0"	.. Telephone Box	East Beach
28	18' 0"	.. Finger Post, opposite "Wi Wurry" Garage	.. ..

29	7' 0"	From Fence, Dunrobin, near Garage Gates	East Beach
30	--	South side of "Happidais"	.. ..
31	--	East side of Entrance gate, Norton Priory	Norton

A directive from the National Fire Brigades' Association (Fire Prevention Department) dated December 1931 indicates quite clearly that owners of large houses should make themselves aware of the best water supply available for their particular location.

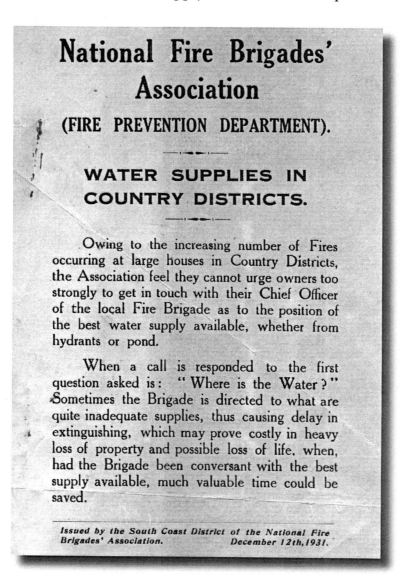

On 26th March 1932, the following letter was received from Westhampnett District Council:

re: Selsey Water Co.

Herewith are two plans, mounted on linen as desired of the Fire Hydrants in the Parish of Selsey.

All those shewn on the plan have been verified. In some cases considerable trouble was experienced in locating them as the roads have been made up covering them.

On my last visit to Selsey I was unable to obtain information as to the length of hose carried so I enquired of Messrs Merryweather, the Fire Appliance makers, and was told the usual quantity carried on a fire hand cart was ten or twelve sixty feet lengths. In colouring the plans, I took the lower measurement viz: 200 yards as showing the area protected.

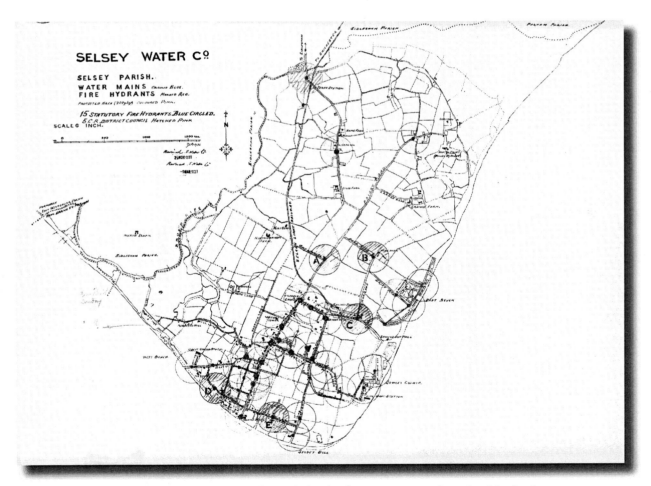

This map, showing the location of the hydrants, was enclosed with the letter

> *I think you will agree that the town is well provided for. I may tell you I am told that Mr Berg at East Beach has his own appliances in case of fire; also at Norton Priory similar provision is made.*
>
> *Yours faithfully,*
> *F J Hazeldine*
> *Director*

The fire hydrants continued to be the subject of discussion, particularly who paid and who owned them. While the Council was waiting for news of their 1932 application for the loan of money to pay for a fire engine, correspondence took place between the Selsey Water Company, the Westhampnett Rural District Council and the Selsey Parish Council, concerning the ownership and the subsequent responsibility for maintenance of hydrants which had been provided over and above the original 15. The Parish Council suggested that at least some of them had been paid for by private individuals. In any case, since they had been installed by the Water Company without any reference to the Parish Council, the latter had no claim over them, nor was it responsible for the hydrants' maintenance. Eventually, recourse was had to the Ministry of Health which, in a statement of 20th July 1932, invested the Rural District Council with the powers to place the expenses firmly at the door of the Parish Council. So ended the hydrant saga.

5 – Keeping the Equipment in Good Order

Neither a borrower, nor a lender be … [8]

In July 1913 the Fire Appliances Committee (formed on 16th April of that year and consisting of Messrs Bromley, Benstead and the Chairman) reported to the Parish Council that they were 'glad to inform the Council that Mr Charles Wingham would undertake the Captaincy of the Fire Brigade, in succession to Mr Cutler'.

Although Mr Cutler had officially resigned in October 1912, he had continued to be involved with the Brigade while a successor was found. The Committee had received the following letter regarding damage to a fire hose:

> *In reply to yours of the 7th inst (July) I beg to say that the hose referred to was kindly lent to me by Mr A J Cutler, builder, of Selsey for the purpose of conveying water from the water main to the water barrel while road-making at Selsey. There was nothing agreed on for the hire of the same and no payments had been paid by me for the use of such hose but recently the Westhampnett Rural District Council have supplied a new length of canvas hose to replace the old one used by me as before mentioned. Yours obediently, signed J J Budden.*

It was also reported at the Parish Council meeting that a letter with a cheque had been received from Westhampnett Rural District Council:

> *Dear Sir,*
>
> *The Rural District Council have been in communication with Mr A J Cutler of Selsey with respect to the purchase of the hose belonging to the Parish Council which was hired by the District Council's surveyor for use in connection with the steam rolling at Selsey. It is alleged that the hose was damaged whilst in use by the Council's employees and Mr Cutler has submitted a claim of £2.13s.0d., being the amount incurred for the purchase of a new hose.*
>
> *The Rural District Council upon the information before it has agreed to purchase the damaged hose for the sum of £2.13s.0d., the amount of Mr Cutler's claim and herewith I send you cheque for this amount, the receipt of which please acknowledge.*

---

[8] William Shakespeare, *Hamlet*, 1600

I shall be obliged if you will give directions for the hose to be handed to Mr J J Budden, the Council's Highway Surveyor upon application.

*Yours faithfully,
W D Rasell, Clerk*

The Parish Council meeting minutes for 15th July 1913 show that, although this cheque was paid into the Parish Council's account, the Clerk had already given his personal cheque for £2.13s.0d to Mr Cutler and was requesting a refund. There is no information about why Mr Cutler should receive the money personally, particularly when it appears to be his fault that the hose was damaged. Mr Budden had stated clearly that no hire fee was requested or paid. Perhaps Mr Cutler bought a replacement hose with his own money.

(It is probable that the Rural District Council in fact paid £2.13s.0d by cheque, rather than supply a piece of hose and that Mr Budden had misunderstood what actually happened.)

The Committee had received notice from Mr Arnell to find new accommodation for the fire equipment. He was accorded a hearty vote of thanks for the use of his storage and told that the equipment would be removed promptly. The Committee had approached Mr Fogden who agreed that the equipment could be stored in his barn. They visited the barn and agreed that it would be very suitable, subject to some minor alterations.

It was proposed that a rent of £1 per year should be offered subject to three months' notice. These terms were accepted, along with agreement that a load of ballast could be purchased to level the floor of the barn.

The Fire Appliances Committee issued instructions to the newly appointed Captain of the Brigade, Mr Wingham and also to Mr Fogden, that in future the Council's hose should be used for fire purposes only and under no circumstances must it be loaned or hired out for any other use.

By 1914 it appears that Mr Wakely, the writer of the original letter of complaint to the Local Government Board in 1910, had now become a member of the Fire Appliances Committee. Further consternation was caused by the discovery that Captain Budden of the Chichester Fire Brigade had inspected the Parish Council's fire equipment without any authority. The Secretary of the Fire Appliances Committee, the same

Mr Wakely, was ordered to launch an immediate enquiry and it transpired that the Captain of the Selsey Brigade, Mr Wingham, had invited Captain Budden 'to come and have a look'. Once again there were signs that the regulations had been ignored when the Surveyor had borrowed a standpipe, so it was again resolved that no part of the fire equipment should be allowed out on hire or loan without the consent of the whole Council.

In 1916 it was proposed that Messrs Barnes, Benstead and Wakely should now constitute the Fire Appliances Committee. Mr Bromley, the previous Chairman, was not mentioned or thanked for his services. All members voted in favour of the new committee except Mr Benstead who voted against, in spite of allowing his name to go forward.

In January 1918, the Clerk reported that a Mr Peacock had offered to sell a manual fire engine to the Parish Council. According to 'Gone to Blazes' - a history of the Bognor Fire Brigade – Bognor Urban District Council sold an old manual engine to Mr Peacock in 1917, for £10. It had apparently spent several years slowly rotting in the Council yard. The Clerk was instructed to acknowledge Mr Peacock's letter and reply that the Council was already in possession of a fire engine.

The Fire Appliances Committee began to be concerned about the state of the fire fighting apparatus. In 1918 they were joined by Mr Sherrington and the Parish Council resolved that they should inspect and report on the condition of the apparatus at least once a quarter. In July 1918 they reported that they had visited the storage place and found that the approach to it and everything stored inside was in a satisfactory condition.

Just over a year later, on Thursday 4th September 1919, a devastating fire at two bungalows near the Marine Hotel in New Road (now Hillfield Road) does not appear to have been attended by the Selsey Fire Brigade and by the time the Chichester Fire Brigade arrived it was too late to do anything other than prevent the fire from spreading further. This was the report in the 'Chichester Observer' the following Wednesday:

Bungalows destroyed

A disastrous fire broke out at Selsey on Thursday evening of last week. Two bungalows being burnt to the ground. The first bungalow was set on fire by a spark from the chimney. It belonged to Mr E Charge,[9] The Cross, Chichester. Both Mr &

---

[9] Mr Charge owned a haberdasher's and milliner's shop which was on the corner of South Street and East Street, Chichester.

> Mrs Charge were out at the time. In a few minutes the thatched roof and upstairs rooms were blazing, then the wind carried the flames to another bungalow belonging to Mrs Walsh with the result that it was soon in flames. In the absence of the fire engine (Having to come from Chichester), people helped get out the furniture besides doing what they could with buckets of water. The vicar worked hard with them and one well-known resident went to the rescue with Minimax fire extinguishers, but the fire had too firm a hold, the only thing remaining to be done was to soak the thatches of other bungalows near, which were in great danger. The fire engine arrived on the scene too late to save the bungalows, but the firemen played the hose on the flaming ruins and so prevented further damage.

A tragic consequence of the fire was also reported:

Fire Sequel

> Mr Meakin of the Marine Hotel lies seriously ill with double pneumonia. He is supposed to have contracted a chill while helping at a recent fire.

Sadly this was followed by an announcement on 17th September 1919:

Death of Mr Meakin

> We regret to announce the death from double pneumonia of Mr R Meakin, son of the late Mr T R Meakin of Anerley at the age of 51 years, at the Selsey Hotel. The funeral took place on Saturday at Norwood Cemetery. Much sympathy is felt for Mrs Meakin.

By now the Fire Appliances Committee consisted of Mr L Maidment, Mr Owens and Mr Wakely and in 1920 Mr Rasford took Mr Wakely's place. This Committee inspected the apparatus once again and this time reported that a section of the hose was in a very bad state and that the Fire Brigade was practically non-existent.

The Council decided that the Fire Appliances Committee should reorganise the Fire Brigade, with the recommendation that it should consist of six men and a Captain and that they should be granted the sum of £1 each per annum for the loss of time taken up by fire practices, which should be at least one per quarter.

The press was still displaying a lively interest in Selsey's Fire Brigade and, on 4th February 1920, reported:

It's a Fire Engine? Great interest was manifest in the village on Monday in the public trial of an elaborate apparatus which one lady described as a new fire engine. It was doing some mysterious work at Mr Maidment's and we are told it will be of decided public utility and a financial blessing to those gentlemen who showed such enterprise in securing it for Selsey.

This is a tantalising revelation as no official documentation has come to light which refers to this incident.

At long last, action was being taken to bring the equipment into good order. The Committee took its responsibilities very seriously and set about the task of reforming the Brigade by sending the following letter to its long-standing Captain, Mr Wingham, dated 13th October 1920. It was perhaps inevitable that retribution would be meted out to Mr Wingham as regulations had been ignored once again when he lent the pump to a Mr Parker of Sidlesham for the purpose of his business.

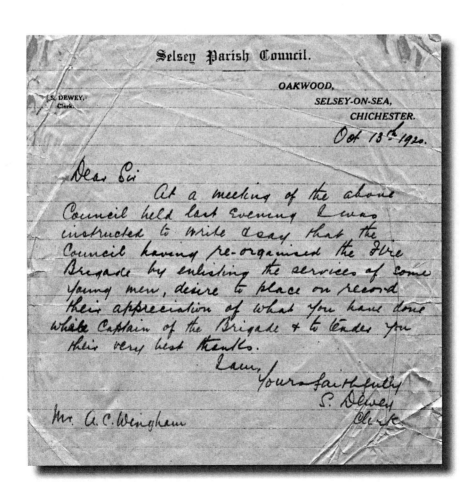

Dear Sir,

At a meeting of the above Council held last evening I was instructed to write and say that the Council having re-organised the Fire Brigade by enlisting the services of some young men, desire to place on record their appreciation of what you have done while Captain of the Brigade and to tender you their very best thanks.

 I am,

  Yours faithfully,

   S. Dewey

    Clerk

This letter brought an immediate, although unusual, reply from Mr Wingham, dated 14th October 1920:

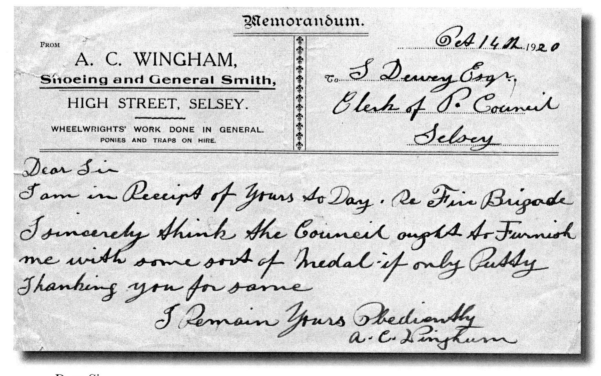

Dear Sir

I am in receipt of Yours today re Fire Brigade. I sincerely think the Council ought to Furnish me with some sort of medal if only Putty. Thanking you for same.

 I Remain Yours Obediently

  A. C. Wingham

An advertisement for a Fire Brigade Captain was posted round the village and a positive response was received:

'Glendelough'
Manor Rd
Selsey
21st Oct 1920

Dear Sir,

In reply to your letter of the 14th October, I wish to say I am willing to act as Captain of the Fire Brigade.

I Am,
    Yours Faithfully,

        W.E. Hellyer

Mr Hellyer's offer was accepted.

6 – Improving the Equipment

Having re-organised the Fire Brigade and enlisted some young men, it's time to upgrade the equipment.

At the beginning of 1921 the Clerk reported to the Council that he had consulted the District Auditor and the Ministry of Health about the payment to firemen of £1 and about the Council's liability in case of accidents involving them. They confirmed that the Council's proposal was permitted under the Local Government Act.

In July 1922 Mr Maidment reported that the Fire Appliances Committee had inspected the equipment and found that two lengths of hose were in a poor condition and that the shortcomings in the equipment made the fire practice useless. It was agreed that the fire extinguishing appliances be put in proper order by purchasing new hose, ladders and other equipment necessary to bring it to a proper state of efficiency. The Clerk was instructed to obtain up-to-date catalogues from Shand Mason & Co. and Merryweather & Co. and to call a Special Meeting as soon as the Fire Appliances Committee had decided their requirements.

Two weeks later Mr Maidment reported that the Committee had decided what they needed to make the Brigade efficient and that the following equipment was required:

	£	s	d
10 50ft lengths 2½" Thistle Brand Canvas Fire Hose, Shrunk and burnettised [approx. cost with fitting couplings and carriage of couplings to Dundee]	46.	10.	0
1 Curricle Fire Escape and Hose Cart with 3 ladders extending to 50ft [approx. cost and with approx. carriage]	13.	0.	0
1 Hook Ladder [approx. cost]	1.	0.	0
80ft Manila Rope ⅝" [approx. cost]	1.	10.	0
1 London Hand pump & 6 Canvas buckets approx. cost	4.	10.	0
Total approx. cost	£66.	10.	0

One of the Parish Councillors, Mr Turtle, reported that he had first written and then paid a visit to the Thornton Heath Fire Station near Croydon and had received the offer of a hose cart and fire escape for the sum of £10. This would be a considerable advantage over ordinary ladders and would be cheaper.

This hose cart, a hand-pushed appliance, became the butt of a series of jokes ten years later, when the villagers debated the possibility of having a motor fire engine (see chapter 10).

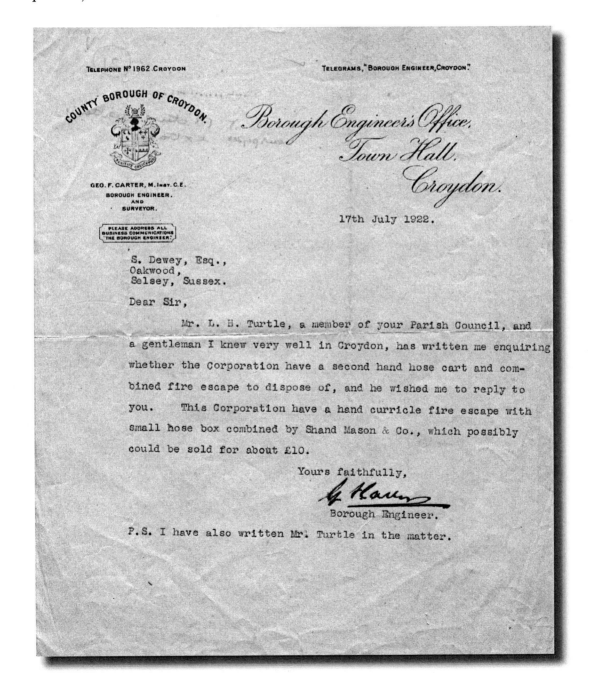

On the proposition of Mrs Gardner, seconded by Mr Turtle, it was resolved that the Fire Committee be authorised to purchase the hose cart and fire escape from Thornton Heath, and the hook ladder, rope, hand pump and canvas buckets as per requisition. The invoice shows what was received from McGregor and Co.

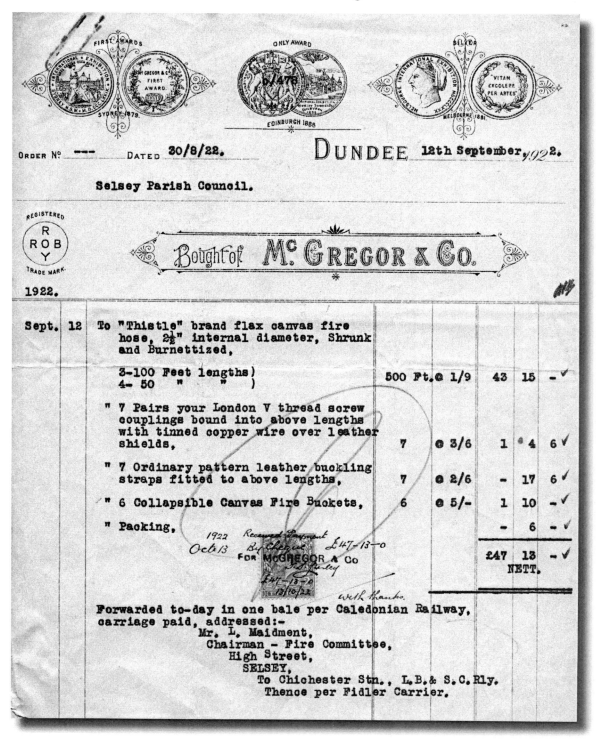

COUNTY BOROUGH OF CROYDON.

JOHN M. NEWNHAM
TOWN CLERK AND
CLERK OF THE PEACE.

Telephone—Croydon 1961.
(Six Lines.)

All Business Communications to be addressed
"THE TOWN CLERK, CROYDON."

J/T.

TOWN HALL,
CROYDON.

19th September, 1922.

Dear Sir,

Referring to the correspondence which has taken place with the Borough Engineer in the matter of the purchase by your Council, of the Fire Escape now housed at the Thornton Heath Fire Station, I have now to inform you that the Committee having charge of the Ex Fire Brigade, have agreed to sell this fire escape to your Council for the sum of £10 (Ten pounds) delivery to take place at the Thornton Heath Fire Station. On receipt of the sum named, the Chief Officer of the Brigade will be advised and you can then arrange with him for taking possession of the escape.

Yours faithfully,

J. M. Newnham
Town Clerk.

The Clerk to the Parish Council,
SELSEY, Sussex.

Although in September a definite agreement had been given by the County Borough of Croydon to sell the hose cart and fire escape to Selsey Parish Council, members of the Fire Committee were not keen to commit themselves to the purchase until they had somewhere to store it, judging by the following report of the Fire Committee on 10th October 1922:

Since our last meeting we have on your authority purchased 500ft of Canons Fire Hose and had this attached in suitable lengths of 50 and 100ft to unions which we had in stock and so have 500ft of perfectly new sound hose in case of fire. We have amongst the existing fire appliances a hand pump. This has been put in thorough working order and tested. Thus, with the six canons, fire buckets purchased will enable a fire to be attacked in its early stages provided a man can be quickly on the spot.

We still require the Ladder Fire Escape but until we have proper accommodation for this we have decided to defer its purchase – possibly lose the bargain offered us by the Croydon Corporation but this we must risk as we have no suitable place to keep it.

We still require a few small matters such as lifeline, hand lamps and new fire helmets – those we have are quite useless except for small boys.

So far we have kept our expenditure within the limits of the budget given us at the last Council Meeting but we are now faced with the difficulty of a suitable shed or station in which to keep our appliances properly and ready for immediate use. As already reported the present place of storage is most unsuitable. The appliances get smothered with dust and it is difficult to get at these, also so many things have to be moved including heavy carts before the handcart can be got out and further, the present Captain and firemen will not take, nor can we expect them to take, any interest for the reason that we have no proper place in which the appliances can be kept clean and tidy and ready for instant use. If a suitable place can be provided we are assured that the Captain and firemen will take a pride in keeping them in proper order and make the necessary drills.

Whilst most anxious to avoid unnecessary expense and have only appliances absolutely essential we feel that as things are at present we might almost be without them – what is the good of appliances which cannot easily be got at and when got at are dirty and the men who are to use them untrained? It simply means that in the case of a fire valuable time must of necessity be lost and possibly life endangered.

We suggest that a suitable shed should be erected as early as possible in the centre of the village at a cost of £50 to £60, the latter figure would include small incidental expenses which at the present we cannot definitely estimate.

We are making enquiries about a suitable piece of ground which may be obtained on lease – quite a small piece would be sufficient – but it will not be until after 16th or 17th that we can obtain particulars on which it could be let to the Parish Council. We quite expect it to be six or even twelve months before this could be accomplished, so that in the meantime we should like to have your authority to secure suitable temporary storage for our appliances. Your Committee have given considerable attention to the matter of providing adequate fire fighting appliances and they hope the suggestions contained in this report will have the serious and earnest consideration of the Council and will give this Committee all the support possible in carrying out what they believe to be really and urgently necessary. We are well on the way to having a proper protection against fire but we can't stop where we are as the money already expended will be largely wasted unless we have a proper place to store and keep in proper order what we have already acquired.

We have been spared a serious fire for some time but one may occur at any moment – let us be prepared for it – we are guardians of public safety and it is our duty to see that we do not fail in this duty – any failure will lay us open to just criticism and censure – if nothing more serious.

Signed L. Maidment

The possible deferment was short-lived because within days a cheque had been sent off to Croydon and a receipt despatched to Selsey, along with the equipment.

CORPORATION OF CROYDON.

BOROUGH ACCOUNTANT'S DEPARTMENT,
TOWN HALL, CROYDON.

No. 6347

17 Oct. 1922

RECEIVED of Selsey Parish Council
the sum of Ten Pounds
for Purchase of Fire Escape
(Thornton Heath Fire Station)

£10. 0. 0.

H. McCall
Borough Accountant.

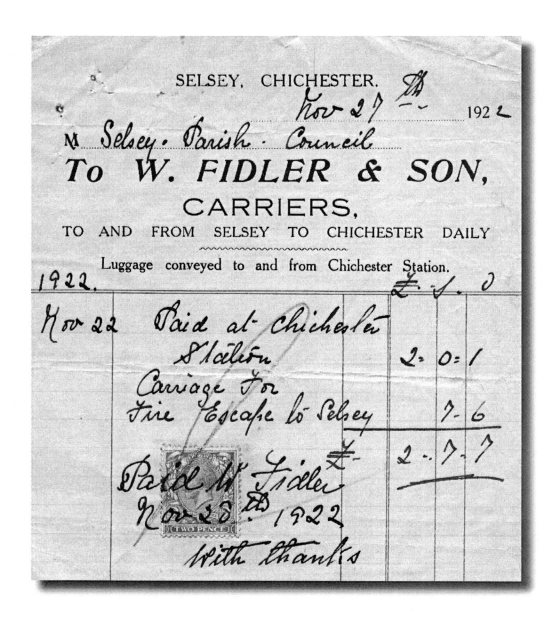

On 9th January 1923 the Committee reported as follows:

Since issuing our last report we have had the Fire Appliances removed from the Barn at Off Licence House to the rear of The Pavilion on High Street – in Mr Phipps' garage and the sign removed and fixed on the side wall of The Pavilion. The whole of the appliances have been overhauled and thoroughly cleaned and put into working order and ready for immediate use. We have now 500 ft of new hose. The Fire Escape from Croydon has been delivered, tested and found in perfect working order.

We regret to report the resignation of the Captain of the Fire Brigade and we shall at the earliest moment elect a new Captain and fill any vacancy on the staff – we shall have difficulties in getting suitable volunteers but the Council may rest assured every effort will be made in this direction.

We have been unable to find a suitable site for this equipment, the only place offered being the back portion of the yard at the side of the barn in the occupation of the tenant of the Off Licence House, for which a yearly rental of £5 is asked. The Committee would be grateful to any member of the Council who can render assistance in securing a suitable site for our Fire Station. They feel that in the future interests of Selsey a piece of ground should be purchased large enough to accommodate a fire station to suit the needs of a larger Selsey, land is sure to be more costly in the centre of the village ten years hence.

The Council is reminded that the present premises in which our fire appliances are stored (whilst a great improvement from the point of easy access) is not considered suitable by any means for a permanent storage place.

On 17th April 1923 Mr Maidment reported that the Fire Brigade needed to be reconstructed as the Captain had resigned and one of the firemen had left the neighbourhood. He suggested that a notice asking for recruits for the Fire Brigade be inserted in the Parish Magazine. By July posters had been issued urging young men to join the Fire Brigade and as a result three or four had handed in their names.

In July, it was also reported that the Committee had still not been able to obtain a suitable building for the housing of the fire appliances and, since the purchase and use of their current site by Mr T J Berg, they had been more difficult to access.

It was suggested that Mr Maidment should be asked whether it might be possible to use part of his new garage as a storage place and it was agreed that the matter of securing a competent Fire Brigade be left in the hands of the Committee and that the emolument be as before.

The hydrant plates had been fixed by Mr Hart, who was paid £2.7s.10d. and the equipment was temporarily stored by Mr Barrow for which £1 was paid. In October the Clerk reported that Mr Maidment was willing to permit part of his garage to be used as a storage place and that the rent would be £5 per year. The question arose as to what particular form of fire alarm should be used and the decision was left to the Committee.

By the beginning of 1924 the appliances had been housed in Mr Maidment's garage and a notice board had been fixed in a prominent position on his house. It had also been agreed that each man should be paid 7s 6d for fire drill practice.

On 19th January 1924 hydrants came to the fore yet again when the Selsey Water Company wrote to the Parish Council informing them that an extension of water mains from the bottom of Station Road (now Church Road), Selsey to East Beach was being made and enquiring whether the Parish Council required the Water Company 'to provide two or three Hydrants fixed on these Mains in case of Fire in this area'. On 22nd January Mr Dewey replied stating that although 'the Selsey Parish Council is not meeting until April…they will at once see the necessity for the insertion of two or three hydrants on the new mains'. He also presumed that 'your company will provide, fix, maintain, renew and keep in order the same at its own Expense as the others already provided in the Parish under Section 28 of the Selsey Water Act of 1907'.

The Selsey Water Company instantly responded: 'According to the Selsey Water Act the Selsey Water Company have provided the requisite number of Fire Hydrants in the district of supply and any further requirements must be provided by the Council at their cost.'

This broadside appears to have fallen on deaf ears as on 18th March the Selsey Water Company chased the Selsey Parish Council for a reply. Unfortunately we cannot relate the final outcome as no further records exist.

On 15th April 1924 the Committee reported that:

> …a fire occurred on Monday March 24th in East Road involving a hay rick, the property of Mr H A Smith. Messrs Maidment and Selsby, ably assisted by PC Pope, turned out immediately the fire alarm was received and to whom the thanks of the owner of the hay rick should have been accorded.
>
> It was found necessary to borrow from Mr Phipps a length of hose as the seat of the fire was a considerable distance from the nearest hydrant. This fact shows that the supply of hose in possession of the Council is none too much but your Committee do not recommend the purchase of any additional hose at present as this is considered an unusual case.

The question may arise as to the water used but until any definite statement is received from the Water Company the matter may be left in abeyance. [It will be noticed that the situation remained the same in 1932, when a similar fire occurred at 7 Council Houses in Beach Road, see chapter 9] *Your Committee are still unable to get a voluntary Fire Brigade together. The question is whether any further inducement of an increased pecuniary nature would induce men to join. We leave it to the Council to consider and decide on this point but your Committee would emphasise the necessity of having a few men who could be relied upon to act promptly should an outbreak of fire occur. It is the first minutes which count in these matters.*

We understand that in the case of any serious outbreak the Chichester Motor Engine would be available but this would mean fully 30 minutes before it can be of any use.

Less than a year later there was a serious fire full of interest and innuendo that brought not only the Chichester Fire Brigade to Selsey but the Chichester police too. We will probably never get to the bottom of what really happened – perhaps a case of 'no smoke without fire'.

On 24th February 1925 a newly built house (sited where 'The Rookery' is now) in Beach Road all but burnt down, as this report in the 'Chichester Post' on the 28th February explains:

Fire and Fine
Selsey Architect's Misfortune
Shrove Tuesday Incidents

Shrove Tuesday this year was an unfortunate day for Mr Frederick Forbes Glennie,[10] the Selsey architect.

In the early morning between five and six o'clock he was watching his newly-built house being burnt to the ground. Five hours later he was charged before the Chichester justices for something wholly unconnected with the fire, and had to pay over £20.

'I don't know where I am at the present time,' he exclaimed later in the morning when he was in the Chichester Police Court. He was charged with not having paid either the health insurance or the unemployment money of eight of his employees.

---

[10] Mr Forbes Glennie designed the Selsey War Memorial which was unveiled in May 1921.

'The Rookery' today, on the site of Mr. Glennie's house

Well Ablaze
Lad awakened by what he thought were rats

It was about ten minutes to five when Cyril Carver, a lad living at no. 1 Station Road,[11] who was due to start work as conductor on the Selsey Tramway that morning, was awakened by what he thought were rats running about. Looking from his bedroom window, he noticed flames coming through the roof of the uninhabited house about four hundred yards away.

Hastily donning a few clothes, he ran to give the alarm. He summoned Mr Glennie from his present home at no. 7 Station Road.[12] Shortly afterwards Police Constables Pope and Boxall, and a few residents who by that time had been aroused, were on the scene of the fire. The house was well ablaze, however, and had been practically destroyed when they arrived.

---

[11] Now 48 Church Road.
[12] Now 36 Station Road.

Very Few Articles Recovered

They set to work in an endeavour to rescue as many articles of furniture as had been spared by the flames. These they took onto the adjoining lawn. In this way, a dinner-wagon, an easy chair, a settee, a case of crockery, some timber and a few smaller things were taken from the building.

Before this was finished, the Chichester Fire Brigade, under Captain Hooper, Second Officer Lewis, and third Officer Weller, which had been summoned by telephone from the Selsey Hotel near by, had appeared. They rendered what aid was possible under the circumstances. Water was pumped from some marshy land in the vicinity, and the brigade succeeded in saving a portion of the west wing.

Superintendent Brett and another policeman from Chichester also came to the village when the alarm was given.

Handsome House
Building Materials from Old Sidlesham Mill

Of Old English design, beautifully executed under the architect's personal supervision, the destroyed house was a particularly handsome building. Many of the materials, including a quantity of old timbers and boulders, were brought from the ancient mill at Sidlesham after its demolition in recent years.

Sidlesham Mill

> *An abnormally long time had been taken in erecting the house, the work covering a period of several years. It was situated in a new road between the Selsey Tramway Station and the East Beach.*[13]
>
> *Mr Forbes Glennie had fully furnished the building and intended to take up occupation during this week.*
>
> *We understand that the damage caused by the fire is covered by Insurance.*

In the record of the Court Proceedings, Mr Glennie managed to produce 'what he said were the Health Insurance Cards', but the unemployment cards were presumed lost in the fire.

The question of fire alarms was also an ongoing saga and, as usual, it took several years of discussion to achieve anything.

The story started on 9th October 1923 when it was reported that:

> *The matter of deciding upon the particular form of 'Fire Alarm' and obtaining of the same was left to the Fire Committee by unanimous consent upon the proposition of Mr Rusbridge and Mrs Gardner.*

Klaxon Ltd, who specialised in supplying factory fire alarms, were contacted on 7th April 1925 and they sent a catalogue with an accompanying letter.

---

[13] This new road was Beach Road and the house was on the corner of Beach Road and Manor Lane. After the fire the house was rebuilt on the same site and was called 'Rookery Nook'.

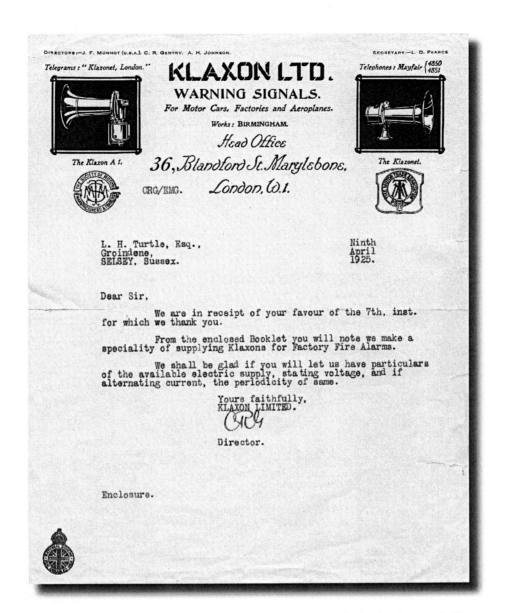

On 18th January 1926 the Fire Committee presented their Annual Report to the Selsey Parish Council in which it was stated that:

> *The Committee recommend the erection of an Electric Fire Alarm at a cost of not exceeding £16. Mr Maidment is willing for this to be erected on his premises without any charge.*

In the end, Klaxon were not directly favoured with the Parish Council's custom. Instead a supplier nearer home was chosen – T F Lummus of 49 South Street, Chichester - although the alarm was still a Klaxon. The order was not presented until February 1927 and the cost was £15 for an HIK Type 240 volts AC Klaxon with cable and suitable press down switch. It was fitted to Mr Maidment's chimney with the switch in a box with a glass face.

7 – The Fire Brigade in Trouble

A lack of firemen means that High Street fires are tackled by 'helpers'

In January 1925, it was reported to the Parish Council that a letter had been received from Mr T J Berg, who, it will be recalled, had purchased Mr Maidment's old garage in which the fire extinguishing apparatus was being stored. This letter claimed £3.10s. for storage of fire hose etc. In fact similar letters had been sent previously and this was the third such letter. The Clerk was instructed to reply and inform Mr Berg that the Council had no agreement with him for such storage and if they had, they would have taken action for the damage caused to these appliances by covering them with cement and by stacking cement in the place of storage, thereby preventing the firemen from obtaining access to the appliances in case of fire. It appears that this reply quenched his financial ambition because there was no further reference to the incident.

In April the Fire Committee had no report to offer and there were insufficient volunteers to form a Fire Brigade. In fact the Rev. MacDermott suggested the abolition of the Brigade altogether and disposing of the apparatus. Mr Rusbridge suggested it should be kept for another year. Mr Maidment offered free storage for the ensuing year, which the Council gratefully accepted.

It seems that young men were not attracted by the appeal for volunteers even with the prospect of 7s.6d for turning out on training nights. At this time the country was in a very deep recession with massive unemployment, so it is doubtful that men in employment would have jeopardised their jobs. Also those on the dole would have had to declare any earnings and so might have lost any other assistance they might be receiving.

Any doubt as to the necessity for a Fire Brigade was soon to be dispelled by a fire which occurred in the following October at Swiss Cottage. The Chichester Fire Brigade arrived 45 minutes after the fire had begun.

The fire was on Thursday 8th October 1925 and on the 14th October the 'Chichester Observer' reported:

Thatched Roof Danger, Serious Fire at Selsey

Another example of the danger of straw-thatched roofs was revealed at Selsey on Thursday morning last, when 'Swiss Cottage',[14] a picturesque little ivy-covered residence, situated in the High Street and said to be over 200 years old, was destroyed by fire.

The cottage was the property of the United Methodist Chapel Trustees and was occupied by Mr W Willshire, a cripple and Miss Willshire, his aunt.

Swiss Cottage

A Mr Reeves, who was passing by the cottage at about 9 am, was the first to discover the fact that smoke and flames were issuing from above the doorway, and he raised the alarm. PC Pope, who deserves the highest commendation for the way in which he acted throughout, was soon on the scene and, with the aid of several willing villagers, attempts were made to overcome the flames by means of pails of water, obtained from inside the cottage itself. This, however, failed to prevent the flames gaining a serious hold, and even the added support of the hydrant and its hose made little difference.

---

[14] Now 66 High Street, next to the Methodist Church. This bungalow, built to replace Swiss Cottage, was worked on by Bill Lelliott's father and was his first solo bricklaying as an apprentice.

> *Meanwhile, as much of the furniture as possible was salvaged and placed in an adjacent hall, but many of the larger articles could not be moved, and were ruined entirely. The furniture, unfortunately, was not insured, although the cottage was.*
>
> *Mr Willshire, who is a tinsmith and tinker, had his tools and other requisites of his trade in a small shed at the rear of the premises, and these were practically all saved.*
>
> *When the Chichester Fire Brigade under Captain Hooper arrived at about 9.45, the thatch was well alight, but in a short time, the flames were subdued, and eventually quenched.*
>
> *A rather pitiful scene was enacted when the fire was first discovered. Miss Willshire was brought out of the cottage, but old Mr Willshire, worried and upset by the suddenness of the calamity that had fallen upon him, refused at first, to leave; and it was with difficulty only that he was finally persuaded to vacate his burning home.*
>
> *Mr & Mrs* [sic] *Willshire had been residents of Selsey for nearly 30 years, and throughout the whole of that time had lived in 'Swiss Cottage'.*

On 13th October 1925 the Reverend A H Boyden wrote to the Chairman of the Parish Council:

> *…to thank all those who rendered such willing and efficient service at the fire last Thursday. Had the fire broken out during the night the consequences might have been tragic in the extreme.*
>
> *This incident shows the urgent necessity of having a local Brigade properly equipped and I believe there are a sufficient number of young men ready to step forth and form a Fire Brigade. Englishmen are always ready to go forth and fight a danger that threatens their homes and if an appeal is made to form this Brigade I am sure a response will follow.*

An article in the 'Bognor Regis Post' of 24th October 1925 stated:

> *After the creditable part played by the brigade of amateur Selsey firemen at last week's fire in the High-street, the Parish Council spent much of its time at last week's meeting discussing the possibilities of re-forming the official brigade which ceased to exist some time back.*

The fire at Swiss Cottage had shown the great need for an efficient fire-fighting body and demonstrated how effective volunteers could be in an emergency.

At the Parish Council meeting held on 13th October 1925, it was reported that two of the Council's hoses were playing on the seat of the fire within seven minutes of the time the alarm was given. All that was needed was a small expenditure in repairing some piping which had burst through excessive pressure from the Chichester Fire Engine at a previous fire in Selsey.

As a result, the Council decided to forward a claim to the Insurance Company for the use of the hoses; for the Fire Committee to endeavour once again to form a Fire Brigade; to reply to Reverend Boyden's letter and to ask him to direct any prospective candidates for the Fire Brigade to Mr L Maidment. The Fire Committee was also asked to submit a scale of fees payable to members of the Fire Brigade and to voluntary helpers when attending fires with the Council's appliances.

Wilkin's and Meade's stores are on the right hand side of the picture

The following spring a small fire between Wilkins, the butchers, and Meade's Stores[15] on 8th March 1926 may not have been considered significant enough to make any request for fees, as no record of any claim for Fire Brigade time was found. A report of the fire was in the 'Chichester Post' the following Saturday:

> *At 12 o'clock on Monday night excitement was caused by fire which broke out in the passage between the premises occupied by Mr H Wilkins and Meade's Stores. The two local constables, PCs Osman and Morris, who were passing at the time, discovered that a box of rubbish had caught fire and had ignited the large double doors. Owing to the promptitude of these two constables and Mr L Maidment, who hurried to the scene with the usual Selsey Firemen's outfit, the fire was soon got under control. Otherwise considerable damage would have been done.*

---

[15] Meade's was a general grocers and was situated in the High Street, opposite the Pavilion Cinema. It was a sister company to International Stores in East Road (now Sell See Beds in East Street).

A few months later, in July 1926, there was another High Street fire, this time at Ellis's, an established grocer (their phone number was Selsey 5) selling a wide variety of goods, which was situated on the site now occupied by a modern parade of shops, by the bus stop to Chichester. No newspaper report of the fire has been found, but a claim was made by the Parish Council on behalf of the firemen.

Ellis & Sons

Anecdotal evidence reveals that in September 1926 surveyors disputed a bill submitted by the Parish Council for £6 after the attendance of the Brigade at the fire, but the following letter shows that the money was eventually received.

21st October 1926 – Letter from Branch Manager, J W L Benaton to Selsey Parish Council:

> 27th July 1926 Fire at Ellis's Bakery.
>
> Referring to the above, we have pleasure in enclosing herewith cheque £2.11s.4d being our proportion of the Gratuities to Helpers who assisted in this case.
>
> Kindly let us have your acknowledgement thereof in due course, and we would add that the balance of £3.8s.8d will be forwarded to you by the Phoenix Assurance Company Ltd.

This was a radical new step in the financing of the Fire Brigade's members, as it placed a precept on the insurance companies, a proposal which less than a month later was put to the test for a second time when a serious fire broke out on 21st August 1926, in the Pavilion Cinema (more correctly known as the Selsey Hall), next to the Crown Public House.

The Pavilion Cinema

On 26th August the 'West Sussex Gazette' reported:

Pavilion Ablaze: A "Cigarette" Fire?

The Pavilion, in High-street, a popular entertainment hall with visitors and residents, is out of commission for many months as a result of a serious outbreak of fire in the early hours of Saturday. The fire was noticed about 4.30 by Mr H Andrews, the baritone of the professional concert party appearing at the theatre, who was occupying lodgings on the other side of the street. Only an hour previously the last of a big crowd of dancers had left the building after a dance in connection with the Golf Club. The raising of the alarm brought the Manager (Mr F W Phipps), the leader of the dance band (Mr Clifford Smith[16]) and others back on the scene just as they were settling down to some well-earned sleep, and the parish fire fighting apparatus was put into operation. Armed with the hose, Messrs. Phipps and Smith pluckily worked close to the now fiercely flaming balcony and roof and succeeded in keeping the fire well in check until the arrival of the Chichester Brigade.[17]

---

[16] Mr Smith also played the jazz drums at the dance and his nickname was 'Darkie'. He was a builder.
[17] The Observer & West Sussex Recorder states that Captain Hooper commanded the Fire Brigade and Superintendent Brett brought a squad of police to the fire.

Although no mention is made of it in the 'Gazette', the 'Observer & West Sussex Recorder' of 25th August 1926 reported that:

> *...Mr Maidment, Mr Bilson, and others speedily got the parish fire fighting appliances to the scene. Water for the hose was obtained from a main near the theatre...*

> *Had the flames not been tackled so promptly their [sic] is little doubt the adjacent inn would have become involved. Falling slates and woodwork made the work of the fire fighters difficult, and Mr Phipps received nasty cuts on the head and hands, which necessitated stitches. With the return of day, the fire was completely under control. The back portion of the theatre, with the stage and dressing rooms, was saved, but the front was severely damaged, a portion of the roof being burnt through.[18] It is thought from the charred embers of several of the tip-up seats in the right-hand corner of the balcony that the fire must have originated here, possibly through a smouldering cigarette end carelessly dropped by one of the dancers. The damage is roughly calculated at about £2,000. It is covered by insurance.[19] The Pavilion was built in 1912 to seat between three and four hundred. It has been under the proprietorship of Mr Phipps and his partner, Mr H A Williams, since 1920. They have run it in a very enterprising way, and much sympathy is felt for them in being thus brought to a standstill at the height of the holiday season. The Rector, Bishop Twitchell, solved the concert party's "housing problem" by kindly allowing them to hold the remaining performance on Saturday night in the Church Hall. Is it not clear that if smoking is permitted it should be someone's job to follow the inevitable stupids who drop lighted matter about?*

The 'very enterprising way' is more clearly stated in the report from the 'Observer & West Sussex Recorder':

> *Good class vaudeville shows, dances, occasional visits from such well-known artistes as Bransby Williams,[20] and during the winter, cinema performances have made the place a popular entertainment centre with visitors and residents alike.*

---

[18] Also, the managerial offices were gutted.
[19] Which did not compensate for the financial loss it meant for Mr Phipps and Mr Williams during the time the theatre was lying idle.
[20] Bransby Williams (1871-1961) worked in the Music Halls reciting monologues and presenting Dickensian characters such as Uriah Heep and Scrooge. He was one of the first variety artists to appear by royal command at Sandringham. He owned a house named 'Elsinore' in New Road (now Hillfield Road).

As this was an extensive fire and came at the height of the holiday season, it was widely reported in the press. The following report from 'The Post' has been included as it differs in some respects from the report in the 'West Sussex Gazette', for example, it seems to be unclear who actually discovered the fire and who called the fire brigade.

28th August 1926, the 'Bognor Regis Post':

A Selsey Blaze
The Pavilion Burnt Down

On Saturday morning, about 4.20 am, a disastrous fire broke out at the Pavilion, High Street, Selsey.

Mrs A Hobden of 'Bryer', High Street, discovered the fire and her elder son went quickly to call Mr Maidment, who, with the help of his two sons, fetched the Selsey Parish fire appliances, while her younger son went to arouse Mr F W Phipps, who, accompanied by Mr C E Smith, and the help of PC Osman, Mr Maidment and his sons, immediately tackled the situation. In spite of the falling slates, melted lead, plaster and timber, they forced their way to the balcony, with the fire raging a few feet above their heads, and were successful in their efforts to extinguish the main outbreak before the arrival of the Chichester Fire Brigade, efforts being unsuccessful to cancel the call, as they were already on their way. On their arrival, they found very little work to do, except for the matter of seeing that there were no further outbreaks.

Great credit must be given to the following who willingly helped to extinguish the fire and thus saved serious damage being done to the surrounding and adjoining properties:

Mr L Maidment, sen., Mr L Maidment, jun., Mr P Maidment, Mr C E Smith, Mr J Bilson, PC Osman, Miss Homer, and members of the 'Delight' Concert Party.

The front part of the building was very badly burnt, including the box-office, right hand side staircase to balcony, and more than three parts of the roof destroyed.

The Pavilion showing fire damage to the roof

During the evening there had been the well-known Concert Party 'Delight', in their performance from 8.15 to 10.15pm, and from 10.30pm until 3am a dance was in progress organised by the Selsey Golf Club, and attended by a large number of people. It is thought that a cigarette end had been dropped or carelessly left on one of the upholstered seats or a window ledge in the balcony, caused the fire.

The concert party were fortunately able to save all their effects without damage, except for being badly smoke-stained, and by the kind permission of the Right Rev. Bishop T C Twitchell, they were able to give their final performance in the Church Hall on Saturday evening.

We understand that the property was covered by insurance with the Phoenix Assurance Co. Ltd.

Much sympathy is felt locally and by the visitors with the owners, especially Mr E D Phipps, part owner and manager, who since taking over the building has provided Selsey residents and visitors alike with varied, enterprising entertainments, far superior to those given in larger towns, such as cinema performances, dances, whist drives, high class concert parties, orchestral and minstrel entertainments, socials, home of the Selsey Women's Institute, for meetings, etc., and available at any time for charitable entertainments of any description, with novel items always at hand from suggestions made by Mr Phipps, who never seems tired of making any enterprise a success.

Although the Pavilion is a tiny building, Mr Phipps has somehow been able to bring star attractions from the London Coliseum, etc., such as G P Huntley and Co., Nelson Keys and Co.[21], on two occasions, the Russian Ballet, Harry Tate[22] and Co., Gwen Farrar[23] and Billy Mayerl.[24]

The auditorium after the fire

The Pavilion is noted for record bookings time after time every seat being booked in the house. We trust Mr Phipps will soon recover from his injuries received during the fire, and are certain his efforts will now be redoubled to get things going again.

---

21 Nelson Keys (1886–1939) was an actor both on the stage and in more than 19 films. He founded Imperial Studios at Elstree with Herbert Wilcox.
22 Harry Tate (1872–1940) was a comedian of the music halls best remembered for his series of sketches on Golfing, Motoring and Fishing.
23 Gwen Farrar was a rather risqué young lady singer, one of her accompanists being Billy Mayerl.
24 Billy Mayerl (1902–1959) was a pianist and composer. He took part in a Royal Command Performance in 1940 and led his own band in the radio programme 'Music While You Work'. He was a band leader well into the 1950s and appeared on Desert Island Discs in 1958.

The 'Observer & West Sussex Recorder' also reported:

The Pavilion

Selsey has certainly come into the limelight or should we say 'firelight' lately. I refer to the Pavilion fire. It is particularly unfortunate that it should have happened in the season, for the visitors will be bereft of their chief source of amusement. Their loss, however, pales into insignificance before that of Mr Phipps, who will lose the best month of the season, and I am sure that his many friends will join in condoling with him over this unfortunate occurrence. From Selsey's point of view, however, there is one 'silver lining' to the cloud inasmuch that it gained a good deal of advertisement, for several of the big newspapers made a special display of it in their contents bills, while all, I think, gave a fairly detailed description. Although the cause of the fire is, of course, not known definitely, it appears to have started in the balcony, which, on the occasion of a dance is used as a gentleman's cloakroom. It is supposed that a gentleman, while changing his shoes or coat, put the lighted end of his cigarette on the edge of one of the plush seats. Additional strength is lent to this supposition owing to the fact that three seats in the balcony are completely burnt out.

The first response by the Insurance Company, Gladding, Son & Wing, was made on 10th September 1926 and stated that:

Mr Phipps has handed us your letter of the first inst., claiming the sum of £5.0s.0d. (Five pounds) for the use of the Council's Appliances.

We would, with all respect, point out that these appliances having been purchased out of the rates, the rate payers of Selsey are entitled to the use of them without payment on the happening of a fire. Therefore, we can make no recommendation for payment of the use of the said appliances.

However, we have reason to believe that Mr Maidment, his two sons, and Mr Smith the builder, rendered services in extinguishing for which a charge might justly be made.

On the assumption that these gentlemen would not object to having their services acknowledged, we would suggest that the amount of your bill be paid to them, and if you concur in this, kindly write to us, when we will make our recommendations accordingly.

In due course the insurance company ultimately agreed to pay the firemen who attended, but not for the use of the appliances. In the case of the Pavilion fire, they paid each man the sum of £1. The six firefighters on this occasion were L Maidment, L M Maidment, P W Maidment, W Hobden, C E Smith and J Billson.

The final press report on the Pavilion fire appears on 9th October 1926 in the 'Bognor Regis Post':

Selsey Jottings

The work of reconstructing the Pavilion has now commenced, but it will necessarily be a lengthy job, as quite three-quarters of the roof was destroyed by the fire, and the date of re-opening is therefore still indefinite. More than one local association will be glad when this commodious building is re-opened. The Bognor Orchestral Society, for instance, which usually commences rehearsals about now, have done nothing as yet and their activities have been seriously hindered by the disaster to the Pavilion.

8 – The Brigade Re-forms

Firemen have a scale of fees for attendance at fires and fire practice

---

At the beginning of 1927 the Fire Committee, in presenting their report, drew attention to the desirability of improving and maintaining the appliances in a state of efficiency. They reported:

> *During the past year these appliances with the willing helpers have been the means of extinguishing two fires which might have proved very serious. As in addition to saving both buildings from being gutted, they prevented the flames spreading to adjoining buildings and property.*
>
> *After much effort the Committee have secured the services of the following to form a Brigade:*
>
> *Captain - W Mitchell*
> *Lieutenant - R Selsby*
> *Deputy - G Williams*
> *Firemen - A Sayers, P W Maidment, L M Maidment, W Head, R Ellis, V Botting, Spen Johnson and B W Marshall.*
>
> *The Committee recommend their appointment, and that they be paid in the following amounts for attendance at fires:*
>
> *Officers - 5 shillings*
> *Firemen - 4 shillings for the first hour and 2/6 for each succeeding hour or portion of an hour, also that they be paid the sum of 6 shillings per Officer and 5 shillings per Fireman for quarterly Fire Practice.*
>
> *The Committee recommend that H Tucker be appointed Caretaker of the appliances, to dry hose and clean and keep in order the appliances after practices, or any fire and that he be paid 10 shillings for each occasion the appliances are used.*

It was also agreed that eight new firemen's helmets, one Captain's helmet and one Lieutenant's helmet be purchased and that Mr Maidment be paid £5 per annum to store the appliances.

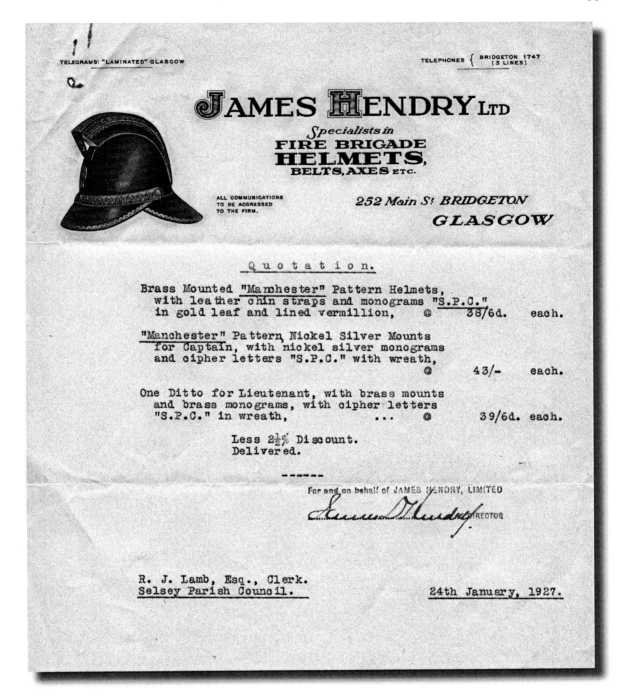

Once the sizes had been obtained (men in those days knew their hat size!), an order for helmets was sent to James Hendry Ltd of Glasgow on 28 February 1927.

Selsey Volunteer Fire Brigade.

		Name	Size
W	E	Mitchell	6 7/8
R		Selsby.	6 7/8
G		Williams.	6 3/4
V		Botting.	7 1/8
B		Sayers.	7
W		Head.	6 7/8
L	M	Maidment.	6 7/8
P	W	Maidment.	7
B		Marshall.	7
S		Johnson.	6 7/8
R		Ellis.	6 7/8

W Mitchell

Feb 22nd 1924

Unfortunately, the demand for helmets was very great and it was only on the 22nd June that Mr Hendry was able to write that the case with helmets on order had been despatched.

It was also noted that an exemption was being sought for Mr L Maidment. As a Parish Councillor he would automatically be disqualified from entering into a monetary contract without such an exemption. An Insurance Policy covering the firemen was also taken out for loss of life or disablement.

The struggle with insurance companies continued over a fire which took place at East Beach on 31st March 1927. A letter from Gladding, Son & Wing requested details showing how an amount of £4.9s had been arrived at before it would pay any claim. They were reminded of the scale of charges agreed by the Council and that the amount of £4.9s was according to this scale, namely:

```
4 hours at 10/-    £2.0s.0d.
5 hours at 9/-     £2.5s.0d.
1 hour @ 4/-         4s.0d.
                   £4.9s.0d.
```

This must have been quite a significant fire when the charges are compared with those for the Pavilion fire (£6.0s.0d) but no trace of it was found in the Press.

At the end of 1927 there was a fire at Mr Thomas Wilson Jenner's at 14 Station Road, (now 22 Church Road). The Fire Brigade attended for one hour, earning the men a total of £2.11s.6d. For the first time there was a claim for two shillings for the hire of a conveyance to carry appliances and a practice earned them a further £2.8s.0d.

Station Road (now Church Road) looking west

January 1928, Parish Council, Report of Fire Committee signed by L Maidment, Chairman:

> *The Fire Brigade received a call at 11.15 am on Monday December 5, 1927, informing them of a fire at Mr Jenner, Station Road and promptly turned out – the Klaxon Alarm acting quite satisfactorily – eight members and the Captain*

(Mr W E Mitchell) being present. The Chemical Extinguisher proved quite effective - the Hose not being required. A serious fire was averted by this very prompt response of the Brigade who were in attendance one hour.

A fire practice was held on the same day and various exercises carried out, whilst these were in operation the <u>Old</u> length of hose burst; it is very necessary that this be at once replaced by a new length, as we have none too much and long lengths are at times needed.

The Committee recommend that the Couplings be at once sent to the makers and a length ordered for quick delivery – a precept will be required for the Fees due to Brigade for a new Refill for Chemical Extinguisher and for the Services of a man for drying and storing the Hose used.

Monday 5th December 1927 – Payment to members of Fire Brigade attending fire at Mr W Jenner's, Station Road, Selsey.

Time of Call 11.15 am   In attendance 1 hour

Present:		s d
W E Mitchell	Capt	5. 0
G Williams	Sub Lt	5. 0
A Sayers	Fireman	4. 0
B Marshall	Fireman	4. 0
P Maidment	Fireman	4. 0
L Maidment	Fireman	4. 0
W Head	Fireman	4. 0
V Botting	Fireman	4. 0
Tucker	Cleaning	10. 0
Messrs Harts Ltd	1 Refill for Fire Extinguisher	7. 6
		£2.11. 6
Hire of conveyance to carry appliance to fire		2. 0
		£2.13. 6

5th December 1927 – Selsey Fire Brigade Practice

		s	d
W E Mitchell	Capt	6	0
G Williams	Sub Lt	6	0
R Selsby	Lieut	6	0
L Maidment	Fireman	5	0
W Head	Fireman	5	0
P Maidment	Fireman	5	0
V Botting	Fireman	5	0
S Johnson	Fireman	5	0
B Marshall	Fireman	5	0
		£2. 8. 0	

On 22nd October 1928 there was another fire in Station Road, this time at H J Hart & Sons. Their yard stood on the site now occupied by Manhood Builders. The report in the 'Bognor Observer' of 24th October stated:

Conflagration at Selsey
Builders' Premises Completely Gutted

One of the biggest fires Selsey has ever known occurred on Monday morning, when a work-shop and premises belonging to Messrs. H J Hart and Sons, the well-known Station Road builders, was completely gutted.

The outbreak was discovered about 11 am[25] and was believed to have originated in the neighbourhood of a stable. The Selsey Fire Brigade were summoned and, quickly on the scene, they worked manfully to subdue the outbreak, which growing in intensity every moment, threatened the little Roman Catholic Church at the side of the premises. Under Chief Officer F Lewis and Second Officer B Hooper,[26] the Chichester Fire Brigade came to render still further assistance, but despite desperate efforts, the fire gained a firm hold, and the whole of the stabling, a workshop, the garages, and so on were consumed completely, the damage done being in the region of £4,000.[27] A large

---

[25] The 'Chichester Post' reports that it was PC Osman who noticed the outbreak and raised the alarm as he was speaking to the owner at the time.

[26] A different document indicates that Mr Hooper was, in fact, the Chief Officer while Mr Lewis was the Second Officer.

[27] In some reports this is £3,000.

quantity of building material was salvaged, however. All the injury that the Roman Catholic Church suffered was to have the whole of the windows on the side nearest the blaze, cracked by the tremendous heat.

Among those who rendered valuable assistance were PS's Bliss and Savage, and PC's Osman and Barnett.

An editorial in the 'West Sussex Gazette', dated 1st November 1928, commented:

Fires and Facts

The disastrous fire at Selsey, reported last week, raises once again the question; ought there not to be 'inquests' into such occurrences whenever the cause cannot be definitely stated? Such a question, of course, does not for a moment suggest that any individual is to blame in the particular instance giving rise to it. In the case of the Station-road fire, indeed, every normal and reasonable precaution against such a danger seems to have been taken. Notices were posted on the premises forbidding smoking – that fruitful source of many 'mysterious' fires – and there seems no ground for any suggestion that this sensible prohibition had been evaded. But when all is said of this or any other outbreak, the fact remains that all fires have a beginning; and in the interest alike of the owner who suffers loss, and of neighbours whose property is at risk, the possible origin of any outbreak ought to be narrowed down as closely as impartial scientific inquiry can narrow it – not to find a victim for blame, but in order that such origins may be guarded against in future. To take a simple example: modern mechanical equipment, either domestic or industrial, especially where electricity is in use, may by some inherent or developing fault easily become a danger to its surroundings. A fire 'inquest,' by ruling out certain causes of a particular fire as impossible, and by indicating, on a careful review of evidence, that certain others may be at any rate possible or even likely, would at last direct attention to the essential facts of each outbreak investigated, and we should get out of the foolish habit of relegating every fire whose origin was not superficially obvious, to the region of the 'mysterious'.

Accidents will always happen, because human contrivance is imperfect, but it is the business of science, when given a chance, so to stimulate human contrivance that its weakest link is always being strengthened.

There was an undated, handwritten note of expenses from Messrs H J Hart & Sons Ltd to Selsey Fire Brigade. An additional note says 'wrote on 7/3/29 for £6–3–0.'

22 October 1928 to Attendance at Messrs H J Hart & Sons Yard in connection with Fire.

Williams G	Deputy Captain	4½ hours
Maidment P	Fireman	4½ hours
Sayers B	Fireman	4½ hours
Head B	Fireman	4½ hours
Ellis R	Fireman	4½ hours
Johnson S	Fireman	4½ hours
Botting V	Fireman	4½ hours
Marshall B	Fireman	4½ hours
Tucker	Getting Fire Outfit in order	10/-

A month later there was an apologetic letter from the Phoenix Assurance Company Ltd, dated 5th April 1929:

22 October 1928 – Fire at H J Hart & Son's [sic]

In reply to your letter of the 4th instant, we duly received your communication of the 7th ultimo and forwarded same to our Fire Loss Dept. for the attention of the firm of Assessors who adjusted the loss on our behalf.

We had assumed that a cheque in payment of your account had been forwarded to you by Head Office, but are writing them today on the subject. We much regret that your previous communication was not acknowledged by us.

On 11th April 1929, there was a receipt for attendance at the fire at Messrs. Hart:

Name		Time Hours	Amount £	s	d	Signature
G Williams	Dep Lieut	4½		15	0	
P Maidment	Fireman	4½		14	0	
B Sayers	Fireman	4½		14	0	
W Head	Fireman	4½		14	0	
R Ellis	Fireman	4½		14	0	
S Johnson	Fireman	4½		14	0	
V Botting	Fireman	4½		14	0	
B Marshall	Fireman	4½		14	0	
H Tucker	(Caretaker)			10	0	
			6	3	0	

A fire at 'Dawn', East Beach (now 97 East Beach Road) on the 31st August 1929 caused another flurry of paper.

'Dawn' is the bungalow with a flat roof and a car parked outside

The fire was reported on 11th September 1929, in the 'Observer & West Sussex Recorder':

Bungalow Fire

It is not often that Selsey is troubled with a fire, and so something of a sensation was caused last week when an outbreak occurred in a bungalow called 'Dawn', at present tenanted by Mr Albert Belcham, on Saturday morning last. Mr Belcham was at breakfast when the first warnings came, and he raised the alarm immediately. Many willing helpers endeavoured to keep the flames under control until the Brigade arrived, but nevertheless considerable damage was caused. I understand that the outbreak as caused by a defective oil-stove in the kitchen.

4th September 1929 – Letter from Selsey Parish Council to Phoenix Assurance Co. Ltd:

Fire at 'Dawn', East Beach on Saturday 31st August 1929

The bungalow 'Dawn' situated on East Beach and owned by a Mrs Sheriff was on fire on Saturday 31st ult. The Selsey Fire Brigade attended and extinguished the fire. I ask that their services be recognised by the usual remuneration. They attended 2 hours and were composed as under:

2 Officers	*@ 5/- per hour*	=	*10s. 0d*
2 Officers	*@ 2/6 2nd hour*	=	*5s. 0d*
3 Firemen	*@ 4/- 1st hour*	=	*12s. 0d*
3 Firemen	*@ 2/6 2nd hour*	=	*7s. 6d*
1 Caretaker & Cleaner		=	*10s. 0d*
			£2. 4s. 6d

6th September 1929 - Letter from Phoenix Assurance Co. Ltd:

Fire at 'Dawn', East Beach

We are in receipt of yours of the 4th instant, but we are returning same herewith as it should be addressed to the owner of 'Dawn' and not to us. So far as we can tell, we are not interested either on the building or contents of 'Dawn'.

The letter is annotated: 'Wrote to Mrs Sheriff, 'Windy Ridge', Manor Road, Selsey on 7/9/29'.

A handwritten note of account was sent to Phoenix Assurance Co. Ltd:

R Selsby Lt	)		7/6
G Williams Lt	)		7/6
A Sayers	) 9.45 -		6/6
W Head	) 11.50		6/6
S Johnson	)		6/6
Tucker			10/-
			£ 2. 4s. 6d

It was annotated: 'King Farlow,[28] Salt Haven, Hillfield Road'.

---

[28] This is probably Vernon King Farlow who also lived at 59 West Street and was connected with the Golf Club.

4th October 1929 - Letter from Sun Insurance Office

Fire – Bungalow 'Dawn', East Beach Selsey. 31st August 1929

We have the pleasure to send you herewith a Cheque for £2.4.6 in discharge of your account rendered to Mrs. Sherriff in connection with the attendance of your Fire Brigade at the outbreak which occurred on the 31st of August last at the Bungalow known as 'Dawn' on the East Beach.

The due endorsement of the Cheque will be deemed a sufficient acknowledgement.

In November 1929 Billy Mitchell resigned as Fire Captain and Ralph Selsby was appointed in his place. It was suggested that the former Chief of the Chichester Brigade, or some other suitable person, be asked to come to Selsey and instruct the Brigade in their duties with a demonstration of the fire apparatus, if possible. This, it was felt, would stimulate interest and efficiency in the work.

A year later there was a rick fire at Coles Farm, just outside Selsey. This farm is the large Georgian house on the right-hand side of the road into Selsey, just before Norton Corner, from whence the Nursery School next door takes its name. At the time of the fire it was owned by Mr Rusbridge, but in more recent times, its owner of many years was George Upfold.

Coles Farm today

The fire was on 24th October 1930, but there is no record of it in the 'West Sussex Gazette' or the 'Bognor Observer'.

An undated handwritten receipt states:

> *Received from the Selsey parish Council the amount as stated against our names for attendance at a Fire at Coles Farm Norton (Mr C Rusbridge) on 24th October 1930.*
>
> *Authority SPC Min Book pp 34 & 35 dt 18/1/27*

Rk & Name	Time	Rate 1st Hour	Other Hours	Signature	Amount £ s d
Capt. R. Selsby	9 hrs	5/-	2/6		1 5 0
Leut L Maidment	1 hr	5/-	-		- 5 0
Fireman P Maidment	1 hr	4/-	-		- 4 0
Fireman V Botting	2 hrs	4/-	2/6		- 6 6
Fireman B Marshall	2 hrs	4/-	2/6		- 6 6
Fireman A Bishop	2 hrs	4/-	2/6		- 6 6
Fireman W Head	2 hrs	4/-	2/6		- 6 6
Fireman S Johnson	2 hrs	4/-	2/6		- 6 6
B Sayers	Cleaning &c of hose				- 10 -
				£	3 16 6

There is a letter dated 5th November 1930, from Gladding Son & Wing to Selsey Parish Council:

> *re- Fire – Coles Farm – 24 October 1930*
>
> *Your account has been sent on to us for attention. Will you kindly let us know which Brigade arrived on the spot first, namely, yours or the Chichester Brigade, and who you were called by.*

(A handwritten note indicates that Selsey arrived ¾ hour before Chichester.)
…and a letter from Wannop & Falconer to Selsey Parish Council followed on 15th November:

> *Policy 2818525-C Rusbridge.*
>
> *We enclose cheque for £3.16.6d in payment of the charges of the Fire Brigade in connection with the fire at Mr. Rusbridges, and shall be glad if you will let us have formal receipt, as endorsed on the back of the cheque.*

9 – Demands for a New Fire Engine

It takes firemen working in their Sunday best, and a hose that's too short, to shame the Parish Council into action

At the end of 1927 Bognor Urban District Council had invited Selsey Parish Council to purchase their old manual fire engine, bought in the 1870s, but the offer was declined. It was over three years later, in March 1931, that the Fire Committee Report to the Parish Council contained a request from the Captain of the Fire Brigade, Ralph Selsby, for the provision of better and more modern fire appliances. Two months later, in May 1931, the question of a fire engine was again brought up but it was unanimously agreed that the subject be held in abeyance until a later meeting … and there it remained for almost a year, until the Council once again faced an embarrassing situation before it stirred itself.

The Press were still interested in Selsey and its Fire Brigade and Captain Selsby was becoming increasingly frustrated. On 30th April 1932, the 'Bognor Regis Post' reported:

Another Selsey Problem
Antiquated Fire Fighting Methods

The time has now come when the people of Selsey must either seriously consider the question of their protection in case of fire, or face the possibility of being without fire protection at all. This was made perfectly clear to a representative of the 'Post' when he interviewed Mr R Selsby, the Captain of the Selsey Fire Brigade.

Astonishing revelations were made at a meeting of the Parish Council the week before, when Mr Selsby stated frankly the parlous condition in which the brigade was.

Our representative asked Mr Selsby what appliances and equipment the Fire Brigade had. He replied that they had 500 feet of hose, one stand pipe, about three or four axes, a helmet each, a push cart for the hose, and a fire escape.

Mr Selsby was next asked what the Brigade had NOT got.

The list was a very long one, and contained some surprising omissions.

The Brigade has not, for example, one fire extinguisher! Should a length of the hose burst, they have nothing with which to repair it.

They have no shovels, no pickaxes, no forks or rakes, no oilskins or any other accoutrements for the firemen.

In the past, it seems that they have had very little encouragement, and Mr Selsby gave our representative a reason for this. The Brigade have not received the support they should for the sole reason that the people of Selsey have not realised the importance of a Brigade, or the havoc which would be caused were a building in the High Street to catch fire during a windy day or night.

Mr Selsby referred to the fire which broke out last year at Mr Rusbridge's Farm [see end of chapter 8], *and said the Selsey Fire Brigade were on the scene when only the outer hay was on fire. 'If we had the equipment', he said, 'we could have saved the whole of the two ricks which were burned, but instead of that we had to wait until the Chichester Brigade arrived.'*

Mr Selsby referred to another instance when only the promptitude of the Brigade saved a large portion of High Street being razed to the ground. A lock-up shop caught fire, the Brigade broke their way in, and extinguished it. 'If we had been half an hour later, four shops and houses would have 'gone west'!'

It will be remembered that at the annual Parish Meeting Mr Hopkins proposed that a fire engine be purchased, Mr Hopkins received no support, and apparently not one member of the twelve firemen was present. Mr Selsby, who was in hospital at the time, knew nothing of the proposition, and apparently no firemen had been made aware that Mr Hopkins intended to make it. Mr Selsby said that neither he, nor, so far as he knew, any member of the Brigade were consulted by the Fire Committee with regard to the proposition, or the purchase of the engine.

'I think', he answered when questioned, 'that a fire engine is absolutely necessary. We have a radius of from two to three miles to cover. It would take the Chichester engine 35 minutes to get here. A few years ago two bungalows, caught fire and were burnt out in 25 minutes. We managed to save one other bungalow, and all that was before the Chichester Brigade could get here.'

According to Mr Selsby the Fire Committee have done little with regard to the purchase of an engine. He made an application for one just at the time the Parish Council were considering the question of the sewerage scheme, and the Parish Council replied that they would get on with the question of a fire engine as soon as they had finished with the sewerage scheme. Mr Selsby pointed out that there were places smaller than Selsey which had their own engines. 'It will be alright till something really serious happens and someone is killed,' he said.

In the meantime, fate lent a hand in the form of a fire at 7 Beach Road on 22nd May 1932.

7 Beach Road was sometimes referred to as 7 Council Houses (This house is now 20 Beach Road). The occupier was Mrs Henry Moore (Sally) and her children Kath, Rita, Ted and John. The girls were at home during the fire and remember how scared they were.

Sally, Kath and Rita in the garden of 7 Beach Road

On Saturday 28th May 1932, the 'Bognor Regis Post' reported:

Selsey Fire
The Brigade Were Willing but – the Hose was Too Short

Another act in the tragic comedy of Selsey's fire fighting facilities was played on Sunday. The village has so far only seen the broad farce of Selsey's inadequate fire fighting equipment, but tragedy might easily be ushered in by a high wind.

But let what happened on Sunday speak for itself.

At 9.40 am, the Selsey Fire Brigade were called out to the scene of a fire which had broken out in a Council house, no. 7, Beach Road, the residence of Mr and Mrs H Moore. They were on the scene of the conflagration at 9.45 – five minutes later – and found that the outbreak was in the back bedroom. Mr R Selsby, the captain of the Brigade, immediately organised a 'bucket party' of neighbours, and sent for the fire extinguisher. A search was then made for the fire hydrant; and it was found in Manor Road, buried in the turf.

The hose was then fixed, **and it was found to be too short by 40 feet!** *By this time, the outbreak had been got under control. The fire extinguisher which was used to subdue the flames* **was not the property of the Fire Brigade, but was borrowed for the occasion from Mr. Maidment!**

The seriousness of the position can be gleaned from these facts, and those that follow.

The fire was caused, it is thought, by the cast iron chimney of a lighted copper fire in the scullery passing the floor boards in the bedroom above, and igniting a doll's house. Part of the bed was burned. Fortunately, there was no wind, and the window was closed. Had it been a windy day, and had the window been open, a terrible blaze would have resulted.

There were nine firemen present. Some of them were in their Sunday suits, and the equipment of the Brigade does not include overalls. The men were forced to risk ruining their best clothes in a task which might have been hopeless.

What attitude will the Fire Committee of the Selsey Parish Council take in face of what many villagers consider a warning? It is impossible to guess, but the fact remains that about five weeks ago the Committee were asked by the Council to meet the Captain *of the Fire Brigade (Mr R Selsby) to discuss the position. On Monday, the day **after** the fire, Mr Selsby received the first communication from the Committee, when Mr Hopkins, the Chairman, called upon him, and asked him what the Brigade required.*

It would seem that the Brigade require many things, for although they were on the scene of the fire within five minutes, they were unable to cope with the fire with their own equipment; the hose was too short; the fire was put out by an extinguisher, and that extinguisher was borrowed!

It is interesting to speculate whether or not this fire would have been reported had not several worthy citizens bombarded Selsey Parish Council and the newspaper with letters of outrage at the state of the Selsey Fire Brigade.

In spite of much discussion about hydrants, it appears that the means of getting the water to the fire had not had top priority, as the following letters to Selsey Parish Council indicate:

23rd May 1932 - Letter from J Berg, Dunrobin, Selsey:

Doubtless you are aware that a fire took place yesterday at no. 7 Council Houses Selsey and the utensils that Selsey is provided with for battling with fire outbreaks was just the laughing stock of the onlookers and had it not been for the Extreme Exertions of the Volunteers and a few of the residents there is no telling, had there been any wind what the result may have been.

I certainly think it time Your Council dealt seriously with this matter so that Selsey can be provided without delay with a proper up to date fire engine and utensils to deal with outbreaks:-

I put it to your Council that at the very worst a penny rate or even less would pay for it – and this before we have loss of life and property.

26th May 1932 - Letter from Luther Clayton, Nortonlea, Upper Norton, Selsey:

I hear you are having a meeting with regard to the out of date and worn out fire appliances. Selsey is a large and scattered place and ought to have up to date fire appliances, so as to get to any fires quickly, before much damage is done and I think it would be money well spent. It has been talked about for years but has ended in talk.

27th May 1932 - Letter from Gordon Jeavons, Grasmere, West Street, on behalf of Selsey Ratepayers Association:

> *I have been requested to write you on behalf of the above Association, to draw your attention to the lack of hose piping for the Fire Engine at the recent fire.*
>
> *Although the locality is a new one, it seems rather lamentable that in a village the size of Selsey, no proper appliances are available and in case of a bigger fire quite inadequate.*
>
> *No doubt this is having the Council's serious attention, and if the Association can help in the matter, please let me know.*

31st May 1932 - Letter from Lawrie Sargeant of the Selsey Hotel (this was on the corner of Manor Road and Church Road and was later called the Stargazer, then the Manor House and has recently been replaced by flats):

> *After seeing the display given with the Local Fire Equipment last Sunday week – opposite my hotel.*
>
> *Do you now think it is about time that Selsey had a proper Fire Fighting Apparatus.*
>
> *The Village has grown rapidly during the course of the last few years, and many smaller places are Certainly better equipped than we are.*
>
> *Should the fire have developed in Beach Road, the present appliance would have proved utterly useless as there was insufficient Hose, in the first place to reach the house, within considerable distance.*
>
> *May I point out that I think it imperative that there should be some means of Mechanical Pressure behind the water, also efficient Chemical Extinguishers.*
>
> *Hoping you, as a Parish Council, will give this matter your most Earnest Consideration, as delay may mean the loss of life and valuable property.*

4th June 1932 - the 'Bognor Regis Post':

> *Selsey Fire – Letter to the Editor from Walter F Hopkins, 'Crossways', Selsey*
>
> Sir
>
> As the article appearing in your issue of Saturday, May 28th, on the fire in Beach Road, suggests negligence on my part in discharging the duties of Chairman of the Fire Brigade Committee, I desire to place my position in the matter before your readers. It is said in the article that the hydrant in Manor Road was buried in turf. If this be correct, the Westhampnett District Council, whose duty it is to supervise the fire plugs, have failed in their duty, in that at the last meeting of the Parish Council the Captain of the Fire Brigade, who was present, when asked if any of the hydrants were covered up, replied that they had all been inspected and cleared. It is true, as stated in the article, that the hose used was too short to reach from the hydrant in Manor Road to the house in Beach Road, but had a further length of hose been added without a fire engine, it would, owing to want of pressure, result only in a trickle of water coming through; to obviate this difficulty the Parish Council have again and again requested in vain the District Council to provide more hydrants, and pointed the danger arising from the present inadequate supply. When they built 40 Council houses in Beach Road, it was naturally expected that a hydrant would be provided by them to protect their own property; however, even this was not done. The attack on myself is a little unfair, having regard to the fact that at two Parish Meetings I brought forward a resolution that it was absolutely necessary to seriously consider the advisability of purchasing a fire engine, owing to our fire appliances being utterly useless to deal with any serious outbreak of fire, but at neither meeting was I supported by the ratepayers.

There was also a letter to the Editor from an anonymous writer although in the light of the last paragraph, it is likely to have been Mr Lewis Maidment.

> Sir
>
> Your comments in last week's 'Post' re Selsey's fire appliances are very opportune, and hope will have the attention of the Parish Council, which they deserve.
>
> Either we should have a properly equipped brigade adequate for the needs of this growing parish, or scrap what we have, then residents would realise that if a fire occurs on their premises they must provide the means of coping with it themselves. This, to my mind, would be a retrograde action.
>
> We have, or had, the elemental necessaries for coping with fire, these should be supplemented by a motor pumping engine, chemical extinguishers for first aid (often

the only aid needed if a prompt response is made to a call), and an addition to the present supply of hose, which was insufficient to deal with the fire you refer to in your comments, and any other really necessary things which the Captain may ask for. Given these really necessary implements we should ensure the enthusiastic services of our brigade, who would, I am sure, take a keen interest in maintaining their efficiency, under their present very able Captain.

We have an effective fire alarm which I was instrumental in having installed, but this is useless unless supported by the necessary appliances.

At the meeting on 13th June 1932, the Parish Council received this report:

Mr W F Hopkins having obtained estimates explained to the Council the approximate cost of a fire engine and equipment and stressed the point that an up-to-date fire engine was necessary for the Parish of Selsey. The Chairman explained what had happened years ago when this question, i.e. of providing a fire engine, was raised. Dr Barford asked what the water pressure would be and Mr Hopkins replied that we could get a pressure of 150 lbs to the square inch. The discussion continued and finally it was proposed by Lt Col W G Moore and seconded by Mr R Smith that a Parish Meeting be called and that the Parish Council recommend that a fire engine and equipment be purchased at a cost not exceeding £1,000. (Does not include equipment.)

The proposal was carried.

Still the Press continued to pillory the Parish Council and on 18th June 1932 the 'Bognor Regis Post' reported:

A Laughing Stock
Selsey's Fire Fighting Appliances
Parish Meeting to be Called

The Fire Committee of the Selsey Parish Council recommended the council at a special meeting on Monday evening, to purchase a fire engine and appliances. Beside Mr S H Day, who was in the chair, there were present, Mrs L Gardner, Lieut-Col W G Moore, Mr Wingham, Mr W F Hopkins, Mr R Smith, and Dr P C Barford, with the Clerk, Mr C E Vince.

Mr Hopkins, in presenting his report, which was a verbal one, said that after considering everything, the Committee agreed to recommend the Council to purchase a fire engine.

Asked to give some idea of the price, he said that a motor fire engine, with attachments, would cost £714.6s. Answering Mr Day, he said that the engine should be paid for over five years by means of a loan which would mean a 2d rate. He said that in the estimates for equipment, the figures quoted were for 12 men, but he considered that eight men were sufficient. He believed that there were at present 12 men in the brigade, and Mr R Selsby, who was present, said that they had 12 men, but did not, of course, get all the 12 at each call.

He referred to an item for two pairs of officers' boots, and said he did not think the officers wanted any better boots than the other members of the brigade. Thirty-three lengths of hose were quoted for, but he thought they only wanted 15, and this would cost roughly £70. In answer to further questions, he said that he claimed to have had a lot of experience with fires, and was not talking out of the back of his neck. Fourteen hundred feet of hose was quite sufficient. Another item was a foam extinguisher. At present they had nothing to put out a petrol fire or anything like that, and this would cost £7.15s. He also said that waterproof jackets were quite unnecessary, and said that the total cost of engine and equipment, including a drying tower, would amount of £935.15s.

The Committee did contemplate having to build a garage, but Mr Maidment had offered garaging for £20 per annum, and also a site for the drying tower.

Another discussion followed upon the strength of the brigade, and Mr. Selsby said that they could not reduce it because they did not get all the men there. 'You are saving £50 on £1,000, and taking off necessary stuff!' he said, referring to items which Mr Hopkins had said were unnecessary. Double-breasted jackets were suggested for warmth, and the officers' boots were lighter ones because they had more running about to do.

On the instruction of Mr Day, the Clerk Mr Vince, here read letters from various Selsey residents, including one from the Ratepayers' Association, all of which urged the necessity of providing a fire engine. One said that the appliances were the laughing stock of the onlookers at the recent fire, and had it not been for the exertions of volunteers, and had there been a wind, there was no telling what would have happened.

Mr Day said that the question came up some years ago, and Mr Maidment, sen. was very energetic about it, and the Council felt they could do nothing until there had been a parish meeting. The matter did not progress very satisfactorily because they had a sewage scheme before the parish which was estimated to cost £50,000 and the council did not think it would be proper to incur another £1,000. At the last parish meeting, Mr Hopkins did bring the matter forward. Forty people were in attendance, and to his (Mr Day's) dismay, there was no seconder. He noticed, he thought, at least three members of the Committee of the Ratepayers' Association present, and not one of them seconded. One of them was putting hostile questions. There was no doubt that the matter fizzled out, and that it was not properly heard. Mr Arnell had given him the opinion that if the ratepayers wanted it, they must have it. He personally could not vote for it at the Council because they would be in a very foolish position, having said that the matter must go before a meeting of the parish, and then vote for an engine after the parish had turned it down. If they intended to apply for a loan, the Council must go to a Parish Meeting. In that respect they were in a good position because they had never borrowed anything at all.

A discussion followed as to the pressure of the water in the present mains, and what the pressure would be when the new mains were completed. The questions were asked by Dr Barford, who was informed that the Water Company would not furnish them with particulars of the pressure in the mains. Answering Lieut-Colonel Moore, Mr Hopkins said he understood that the fire engine (cleaning, etc) would be maintained voluntarily by the Brigade. In reply to a further question from Colonel Moore, he said they received £10 and all costs for each fire attended.

Col. Moore moved that a special meeting of the parish be called, and that the Parish Council recommend it to purchase a fire engine and equipment at a cost not exceeding £1,000.

The question of training was raised by Mr Hopkins, and Mr Selsby said that the Chichester officers would be only too pleased to come down and tell them all they knew. Mr Smith seconded the resolution, and Dr Barford moved an amendment that the matter be delayed till the pressure in the new supply of water could be ascertained.

Mr Hopkins was referring to the probable income from the fire engine, when Mr Day interposed. 'I think you are being a bit of an optimist. The next thing we shall do is to declare a dividend!'

On being put to the vote, six were for the proposal. Mrs Gardner did not vote.

It was decided to hold a Parish Meeting on Monday, June 27th, at eight o'clock in the Church Hall.

NOTICE.

A PARISH MEETING

WILL BE HELD AT

CHURCH HALL SELSEY

ON

Monday, June 27th

AT **8** p.m.

Agenda
MINUTES.

Fire Engine

By order

[signature] Chairman S.P.C.

C. VINCE, Clerk to the Selsey Parish Council.

NOTE—Only "LOCAL GOVERNMENT ELECTORS" are eligible to attend and vote.

MOORE & WINGHAM, PRINTERS, 39 EAST STREET, CHICHESTER

1932

10 – Making the Decision

The Parish Council fiddle with loans while the hayrick burns

The Parish meeting was duly held and on 2nd July 1932 the 'Bognor Regis Post' gave this comprehensive report:

Selsey's Fire Problem
Necessity of Adequate Appliances
Important Decision at Parish Meeting

The ratepayers of Selsey, as represented by the fifty odd who attended the special Parish Meeting, called by the Selsey Parish Council, on Monday, in the Church Hall, to consider proposals for the purchase of a fire engine and equipment, voted overwhelmingly in favour of buying one. Mr S H Day, as Chairman of the Parish Council, presided, and he was supported upon the platform by Mr W F Hopkins (Chairman of the Fire Brigade Committee), Lieut-Colonel W G Moore, Mr R Selsby (Captain of the Fire Brigade), with Mr C E Vince, acting as Clerk. Among those present were Mr E Heron Allen, Chairman of the Water Company.

Mr S H Day, in a brief explanation as to why they were there that evening, said that some years ago Mr Maidment, an energetic member of the Parish Council, was very much in favour of having a fire engine, and the Council were in favour of the scheme, but had no power before they had taken the proposal to the parish. The matter drifted on, because it was found that there was a difficulty about hydrants. Then another difficulty arose in the sewerage scheme, and the Council thought it was useless to ask the parish to spend £1,000 on a fire engine when it might have to spend £50,000 on a sewerage scheme.

At the last Parish Meeting, Mr Hopkins brought the matter forward, but it terminated very unfortunately. There was no one present to second it. It was most unfortunate that Mr Selsby was laid up at the time. After that there was a fire in Beach Road, and as a consequence of this letters came to the Parish Council (some of which were rather indignant), and Mr Hopkins and Mr Selsby called upon him (Mr Day) and said something must be done. He told them that the Parish Council could not deal with it before a Parish Meeting. The Parish Council were all in favour of holding the meeting.

'It is for you to say whether you want it or not,' said Mr Day, in conclusion. *'The Council are quite willing to carry out your wishes.'*

Mr Hopkins moved that Selsey have a motor fire engine to replace the 'utterly useless fire appliances at present in stock'. As Chairman of the Fire Brigade Committee, he thought it was his duty to place before them the facts relating to the disastrous state of the brigade and appliances. Referring to his credentials, Mr Hopkins said that during the War, as a volunteer, he attended upwards of 200 fires as a member of the London Fire Brigade. He went through the County Council School, passed the examination, and was awarded a first class certificate. Soon after his election on the Committee, he made it his business to call upon Mr Maidment and ask to see the appliances. He had no knowledge of what they possessed, and assumed that they had a manual engine. He was shown a few lengths of hose and a stand pipe. That was all they possessed, and they were paying £5 a year for its storage. In reply to further questions, Mr Maidment told him that they had nothing with which to dry the hose, but generally placed it on old motor tyres. 'On the pictures, that would be very funny', commented Mr Hopkins, 'but to the ratepayers of Selsey it is more serious'. He referred to the difficulties in drying the hose under these conditions, and the damage which must necessarily follow. For these appliances they paid £25 per annum, so they could see the matter was serious.

When leaving he spotted something else. He was told that it was the fire escape, and when asked if it was any good, Mr Maidment replied that it was not. It had been there a number of years, and they had not used it. 'I am not an authority on antiques', commented Mr Hopkins, 'and I asked how it came into the possession of Selsey. I have been unable to ascertain the date of its birth or the period, but it once belonged to Croydon, who after using it for a great number of years, decided to scrap it, and ordered it to be placed on the dump. A certain gentleman, hearing of this, had a brainwave, and said: 'That's just the thing for Selsey'. Perhaps he thought a few years at the seaside would help it regain its lost youth'. [The story of the Croydon fire escape is told in chapter 6]

Mr Hopkins referred to the fact that he had brought the matter before the last meeting of the Parish, and said that the warning he then sounded resulted in several residents writing to the Parish Council and endorsing his views. He alluded to the fact that it was reported that the fire in Beach Road was put out with the aid of a borrowed extinguisher, and said it might be funny to outsiders, but it was not very nice for residents to read about. Had the fire been serious, the brigade could have done nothing but watch it burn itself out. Selsey was large and widely scattered, and contained a lot of valuable property.

Held up to Ridicule

The brigade, he said, were a willing body of men, but could they expect them to push the hand truck all over Selsey and then perhaps find that their efforts had been in vain? He referred to their lack of personal equipment, and said that they received little or no remuneration for their services, and on top of all that they were held up to ridicule in the Press because of their equipment.

Lieut-Col. Moore said that he was very happy to second the proposition. He pointed out that the nearest fire engine was eight or nine miles away, and the distance was so great that it made it almost useless to call upon. They had to make up their minds that night whether they were going to have an engine at all. They were labouring under a sense of false security to think that they had fire appliances at the present time, because they had not.

Mr Hopkins pointed out that it might happen that Chichester when called upon might be engaged upon a fire in their own district. Dealing with the cost, he said that he had an estimate for a trailer at £400, but the other was a motor fire engine at £714.6s. He had prepared estimates for ten firemen, and it worked out altogether at £901.18s.

Before this meeting, Mr Maidment had already written to say that he was willing to provide garage space for a new fire engine and space for equipment.

On 6th July 1932, there was a further account in the 'Bognor Regis Post':

Selsey Day by Day
Selsey's Fire Engine

The inhabitants of Selsey really seem on the right road to having a much-needed fire engine at last. Two interesting demonstrations were given by Ford and Morris engines on Monday and Tuesday consecutively. Large crowds gathered to watch the displays, and credit is due to the Selsey Fire Brigade, who give their services entirely free, for the benefit of the population of Selsey.

It is rumoured that engines of other makes will be given a trial, and it is to be hoped that it will not be long now before Selsey has the necessary engine and equipment for future occasions of fire.

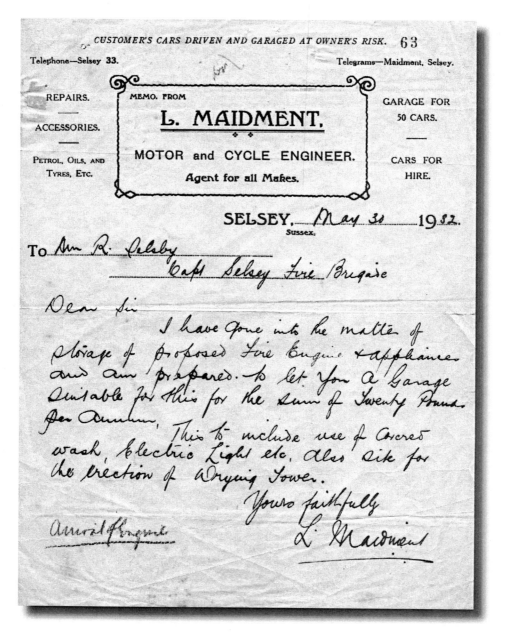

Mr Maidment's Offer Letter

Demonstrations were also forthcoming of Merryweather and Dennis engines.

The news of the application soon became public and in this time of depression £1,000 was a large sum, especially for a small parish council. Several financial institutions of the City of London offered a loan for this amount, which is indicative of the state of the financial world at this time of depression. For most of us this would represent the cost of two or perhaps three new houses.

For example, Charles Seymour Taylor & Co of Mansion House Chambers wrote offering a loan of £1,000, as did the London & Westminster Properties Company and F C Bailey of Basinghall Street. These loans were in the same terms except that one quoted $3^5/_8$%, while others gave no indication of their terms.

>   475-6 Mansion House Chambers,
>   20, Bucklersbury,
>   London, E.C.   26th July 1932.
>
> The Clerk
>   Selsey Parish Council
>   Selsey, Sussex.
>
> Dear Sir,
>   re LOANS.
>
>   We observe that your Council will be requiring a Loan of £1,000 for a Fire Engine. We shall be pleased to make an offer for the amount, and if you will kindly favour us with full details of the security &c, we will send you a Tender for consideration.
>
>   Yours faithfully,

On 16th July 1932 the 'Bognor Regis Post' reported:

> *(Extract from report of Selsey Parish Council meeting held at the Infants' School on Monday night). Mr Day took the chair and among those present were Mr S B Arnell, (Vice Chairman), Mrs L Gardner, Mr A C Wingham, Major R J Lamb, Mr R Smith, Mr W Llewellyn White, Dr P C Barford, Lieut-Colonel W G Moore and Mr W F Hopkins; with the Clerk, Mr C E Vince (Mr R Selsby, Captain of the Fire Brigade, was among those who watched the proceedings.)*

Under the heading of 'Fire Engine', Mr Day gave a brief résumé of what had already happened, and Mr Arnell said that the next thing was to find out what terms they could get for a loan, and submit it to a Parish Meeting.

Mr Day said that they must get the approval of the Ministry of Health, and must suggest the duration of the loan.

Major Lamb: Can we rely upon getting the loan?

Mr Day replied that they could not be sure, but there was no reason to think it would be refused. They had not approached the County Council on the matter until they had something to approach them with.

Mr W Llewellyn White: Will you tell us something about the pressure?

Mr Hopkins: The water pressure does not enter into it at all. You are dealing with a suction pump. As long as there was water there they could put the pressure on by means of a controlling valve.

Dr P C Barford said that they had undertaken this matter at a stage in the Selsey water supply which would change in the near future. When the Water Co. first supplied Selsey there were few houses upon it, and the supply was then adequate. As the consumption increased, the pressure went down, and was hardly adequate to supply Selsey, and was obviously inadequate to supply a hose. They must have a fire engine or adequate pressure in the pipes. It seemed to him very wrong to settle the matter till they knew what difference the new mains would make in the pressure of water. It would be much better to postpone it till they ascertained what the pressure would be under the new regime, and he moved an amendment to that effect.

Dr Humphrys, in seconding the amendment, said he was quite in agreement with Dr Barford. He did not think they should decide till they knew what the pressure would be when they got the extra pipes.

Mr S B Arnell said they had had very efficient work from the brigade in the past. He could call to mind two or three fires which were got under control and practically put out before the Chichester Brigade arrived. The Brigade wanted an engine. He did not know, but he had a strong idea that if they did not provide them with more efficient appliances they would cease to have a brigade (Clapping and applause).

Mr Selsby pointed out that two cottages were burned down in 25 minutes and it took the Chichester Brigade 35 minutes to get to Selsey.

Mr Keep said that if the pressure was all right, he hoped that several firms would be given the opportunity of demonstrating, to see what the various engines would do, and so as to give the most efficient service to Selsey.

Mr Swindell felt very strongly that Selsey had been very fortunate in the matter of fires, but they did not know whether that good fortune would always be with them. He thought there was always a very great risk of fire in Selsey, with so many houses and bungalows, with oil lighting and cooking apparatus. It was little understood by visitors to Selsey, and they had numerous instances of very slight fires caused by them. There might come a day where the fire, fanned by a strong breeze, might get a big hold, and that in some districts would be a disaster.

Another ratepayer pointed that that those who opposed the purchase of a fire engine had not suggested what they should have in place of it.

Dr Barford agreed completely that they must have adequate pressure or a fire engine. There was further discussion with regard to the pressure, and this was closed by Mr Heron-Allen.

He said that he had no idea of taking part in the discussion, but as Chairman of the much abused Water Company he would like to point out that they could not have in Selsey a direct pressure which was reliable at all hours of the day or night. If they arranged to have their fires early in the morning, he would guarantee all the pressure they wanted, but if they were foolish enough to have them in the afternoon or evening, when 150 young ladies had had 150 baths, the pressure would be very unreliable. There was only one way in which Selsey could protect itself against fire, and that was to attach a pumping engine on the existing mains, and that was simply a question of expense, but to talk of the possibility of twenty-four hours reliable pressure from Chichester to Selsey was scientifically impossible.

After this 'authoritative word', both Dr Humphrys and Dr Barford agreed to withdraw the amendment, and the resolution to purchase a fire engine at a cost not exceeding £1,000 was passed by 44 votes to three.

The question of a loan, and the period over which it should be extended, was next discussed. Mr Day said that five years seemed a little short. Dr Humphrys agreed and

Mr Francis moved that the loan be spread over ten years. Mr S B Arnell seconded, and Mr Llewellyn White asked for something more definite as to what rate this would entail. They had not only to repay the interest, but the capital. Having regard to the very indefinite financial statement, he thought the Parish Council ought to call another Parish Meeting so as to give the parish a definite idea as to what it was committing itself in the way of loans. He moved the Parish Council go into the financial side of the project and call another meeting. He was seconded by Mr W Prior and the proposition was carried by 34 votes to 14.

About this time a rather tongue-in-cheek letter from Edward Heron-Allen appeared in the same paper:

Urban Powers for Selsey and Protection from Fire

(To the Editor)

Sir, These two questions are always to the fore, and have never been more so than at the present time. The one is closely bound up with the other, as I propose in this note to show. Chichester is about 30 feet above sea level; Selsey is about 10 – so we get a fall, upon which pressure depends, of about 20 feet in nine miles. This is obviously not enough for the water mains to have enough pressure to throw a stream of water in Selsey to a height approximating that of Chichester. What is the remedy?

We are told that with Urban Powers, Selsey will be omnipotent in such matters. Therefore the first thing that Selsey must do is to obtain urban Powers. It can then promote a Bill in Parliament to raise the whole City of Chichester about 30 feet. But this would be an expensive matter, involving a rate, the mere thought of which causes the brain to reel and the senses to gape. A better and far cheaper plan would be to lower Selsey about 30 feet. This would merely involve rebuilding Selsey into a waterproof concrete tank to that depth. The pressure upon the mains would then be quite enough to enable the Selsey Fire Brigade to deal with any ordinary fire that is likely to occur.

The only danger and difficulty that I can see is that an abnormally high tide might come over the seaward wall of the Selsey-containing tank. In that case all the fires in Selsey would be at once extinguished, but, from what one is told, the municipality of Selsey would be quite able to cope with an emergency of this kind.

The Parish Council now set in motion the paper trail leading to the actual purchase of a fire engine. Initially it needed the approval of West Sussex County Council.

Letter to J E Seagar Esq., Clerk West Sussex County Council, Chichester, dated 13th July 1932:

> *Dear Sir,*
>
> *Purchase of Fire Engine*
>
> *I am instructed by the Selsey Parish Council to make application to the W.S.C.C. for their consent to a loan of £1,000 to purchase a Motor Fire Engine and Equipment and suggest that the duration of the loan will be not less than ten years.*
>
> *I attach certified copies of resolutions which were passed at a Parish Meeting held at Selsey on 13th June 1932 and a Parish Meeting held on 27th June 1932 for your information.*

This produced the following response from Mr Seagar:

> *I acknowledge the receipt of your letter of the 13th instant which will be submitted to the Finance and General Purposes Committee of the County Council at their next Meeting.*
>
> *Your application has unfortunately been received too late for this quarter's meeting and, in the ordinary course, the next Meeting of the Committee will not be held until 11th November.*

Despite this, no time was lost in seeing examples of possible fire engines.

While everyone was enjoying the interest shown, the hand cart from Croydon was still being dragged around the streets, as indicated below in the 'Selsey Notes' report regarding a burning hayrick at Fish Shops Farm (also called Beacon Farm) on 17th August 1932.

On 24th August 1932, the 'Observer & West Sussex Recorder' reported:

Rick Fire

> *The Selsey Fire Brigade received a call on Wednesday afternoon, at about 4.50 to a rick on the Selsey Estates, near the Albion Hotel* [now the Lifeboat Inn]. *On arrival, they found the rick well alight, and at 5.30 the Chichester Fire Brigade were*

notified, and made an extremely smart turn out, but were unable to save the rick, which was practically burnt out.

Co-incidentally, a reporter was in town and he spotted the fire engine on its way to the fire. In the same edition of the paper he made his feelings quite clear!

Selsey Notes by 'Beadle, Jun.'

The Fire Engine

I was in Selsey on Wednesday last, when the fire siren went off in a very businesslike manner. Crowds began to collect, the acrid odour of smoke made my nostrils smart – and still the siren went on. I strolled down the road, trying to get away from the noise that was pursuing me like a hateful demon. Nearly a quarter of an hour went by; abruptly the noise ceased. And suddenly a break-down van, towing a little red box on wheels, came along at quite 15 miles per hour! I watched it out of sight, and then waited for the Fire Brigade. 'They're a long time turning out,' I said casually to a passer-by. 'They're out,' he replied scornfully. 'Didn't you see them go?' 'You mean – that little red box arrangement?' He nodded. 'Of course I do. That's the Selsey Fire engine.' He was most annoyed when I laughed. However, that set me thinking hard. Is it fair to Selsey property owners to have to help pay for the upkeep of a machine that is inadequate to extinguish a bonfire? Is it fair to the firemen to make themselves a laughing stock every time they turn out? Is it fair to Cicestrians to have their up-to-date Brigade and engine travel several miles to a fire, leaving the City at the mercy of any fire that might occur? If Chichester have to attend fires several miles away, they should have more than one fire engine to cope with any other fires that may break out in this very large district. And if Selsey wishes to keep its firemen, it should provide them with a fire engine, for, apart of the existing 'equipment' being ridiculously antiquated, it is hopelessly inadequate for even a rick fire, as instanced on Wednesday last.

Early the following month a letter was sent to the Parish Council which was signed by all the members of the Brigade:

Gentlemen,

I beg to report that the Fire Brigade answered a call to Fish Shops Farm, the property of Selsey Estates, to a rick fire at 5pm on Wednesday, August 17th. On arrival we found rick well alight and as we were unable to do much with one hose, Mr Mason, Estates Manager, called the Chichester Fire Brigade, whose Chief Officer, however, refused to couple up. We were obliged to let rick burn out but two firemen in turn stood by in case of the wind freshening and causing fire to spread to adjoining property. After seeing all safe the Brigade finally returned to Station on Sunday morning. Total hours on duty 83.

Firemen present:
R Selsby (Captain)   *P Maidment*
S Johnson   *Harman*
F Head   *Clough*
W Head   *J Mitchell*
A Bishop   *J Lee*

On 8th September 1932, the 'West Sussex Gazette' was able to report:

Set Fire to a Hayrick

Two small Selsey boys were bound over by the County Magistrates at Chichester on Monday for, on August 17, maliciously setting fire to a hayrick at Selsey, the property of the Selsey Estates, Ltd., valued at £50. William Page,[29] general labourer, of Selsey, said he saw two boys and a girl playing round the rick. One of the children picked up a piece of paper and ran round the rick. 'Witness then saw smoke going up. He shouted to them, and they ran away. Witness tried to put out the fire and then sent for the Fire Brigade.' PC Osman said the defendants made statements to the officer that pieces of paper were lighted and applied to the rick. One of them also stated that some lighted paper was put into a boat, but it did not catch fire. As the fathers of the boys were out of work the Bench remitted the costs of £1.

This would seem to have been a reasonably straightforward affair – a rick fire started by children. However, as Selsey-on-Sea Ltd was involved, it soon became contentious. It would appear that Selsey Parish Council decided to send the Fire Brigade bill to Selsey-on-Sea Ltd as Fish Shops Farm was their property.

The correspondence rumbled on for more than a year. Two of the letters survive:

14th August 1933 - Letter from Wyatt & Son to Selsey Parish Council

---

[29] William Page was a relative of John Ayling and lived at either 28 or 30 Albion Road.

Selsey Estates

We are in receipt of yours of the 12th inst; being account of charges for the Fire Brigade attending the fire at East Beach.

We do not think, however, that this should be a charge against our Clients seeing that the only reason the Brigade was called was on account of the impending danger to the adjacent Bungalows.

Actually no damage was being done to our Clients property, but if the fire had not been taken in hand, we feel sure that some of the Bungalows would have been burnt. We do not know whether you are aware that one Bungalow actually started to burn, but this was quickly extinguished.

We feel that the charge should be one against the Parish and not against our Clients, and shall be glad to hear further from you on the matter after our letter has been brought before your Council.

20th October 1933 - Letter from Wyatt & Son to Selsey Parish Council:

We acknowledge receipt of your letter of the 17th inst. and are surprised to learn the attitude adopted by your Council.

We are still of the opinion that this charge should be one against the parish and not against ourselves.

Surely we should have had notice that the matter was being brought up at the last meeting, when we should have thought we ought to have been given the opportunity of expressing our opinion to the meeting.

In your letter you state that the Council are of the opinion that the fire on the property in question was becoming a menace to the other property owners, and this is the very point on which we think the whole matter turns.

We are only responsible for our client's property and not that of other people.

11 – A New Fire Engine is Finally Acquired

- after waiting nearly a year for the loan to be agreed

At last the Parish Council had made the decision to purchase a fire engine, and to this end requested a quote from Dennis Bros Ltd of Guildford.

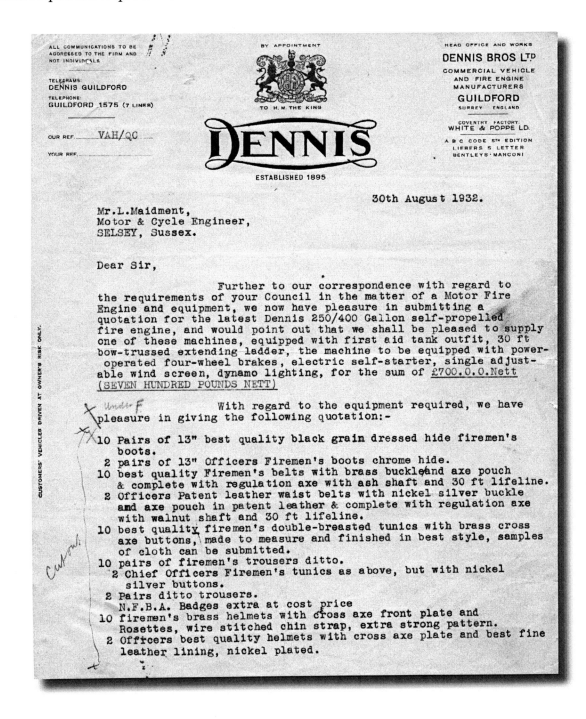

12 pairs of black oilskin leggings.
12 Black oilskin long coats.
34 - 50 ft lengths of 2½" 24 strand pure flax canvas hose, shrunk and burnettized as sample enclosed, guaranteed to stand 400 lbs pressure and made to the L.F.B. specification, with instantaneous couplings bound and rivetted in with tinned copper wire over leather shields, and complete with best quality leather buckling strap with brass Marshallay buckle.
4 2½" polished copper and gunmetal fire branch pipes 15" long ½" jet.
One 5/8" spare jet)
One 3/4" ditto)
One 1" ditto)
One 1⅛" ditto)
One patent adjustable nozzle.

One fan spreader for branch pipe.
Six hose clamps
One hose repairing outfit
One 2-gallon Foam type fire extinguisher complete with finger brackets for keeping upright,
One 2-gallon Soda Acid chemical fire extinguisher.
One 2-pint C.T.C. extinguisher complete with bracket and filled, brass finish.
One first-aid outfit complete in box, large size.
Two Preventer or ceiling hooks 7'6" with gunmetal head.
Two standard pattern pitch forks.
1 Shovel
1 long handled pick axe.
1 gunmetal adaptor 2½" instantaneous x Vee thread, A.on loose sheet.
1 double female instantaneous adaptor 2½" H.
1 double male ditto F.
1 2½" polished gunmetal instantaneous collecting breeching.
2 ditto dividing breechings.
2 Handy Respirators in Pouch.
FOR THE SUM OF £262.10.0.(TWO HUNDRED & SIXTY TWO POUNDS 10/-)

You will note that the total price of the Engine and Equipment, works out at £962.10.0.

The engine which we are bringing down for demonstration on Thursday next, is identical with regard to equipment, to the one quoted for above, and we would point out that should your Council care to consider the purchase of the actual engine demonstrated, we are prepared to supply this machine at the nett sum of £625.0.0. (SIX HUNDRED & TWENTY FIVE) which would bring the total for the above machine and equipment to the nett sum of £887.10.0.

In connection with this latter machine, we would point out that this Engine has all the bright work chromium plated and in view of the fact that this chromium plating costs us approximately £30.0.0.nett, we are offering this machine to your Council at a very special price, and we feel sure that as the engine would be to all intents and purposes new, and would carry our usual guarantee as with a new machine, therefore the Council will give this appliance their very serious consideration.

No doubt, by the time this letter arrives, you will be in receipt of the posters for displaying, and we feel sure that you and Mr. Selsby will see that these are distributed to the best possible advantage.

We are arranging for the engine to be on view in Selsey at 2 p.m. on Thursday of this week, and the writer will be glad to discuss any points with you which may arise.

Assuring you of our interest and best attention at all times,

    Yours faithfully,
    DENNIS BROTHERS LIMITED.

    Fire Department.

The demonstration model would cost £625 and clothing and equipment was estimated at £262.10s.0d. While this was being considered the County Council approved in principle a loan of £1,000 for the fire engine and equipment and an application would be made to the Ministry of Health accordingly if the Council agreed.

The Fire Committee had also sought estimates from other companies.

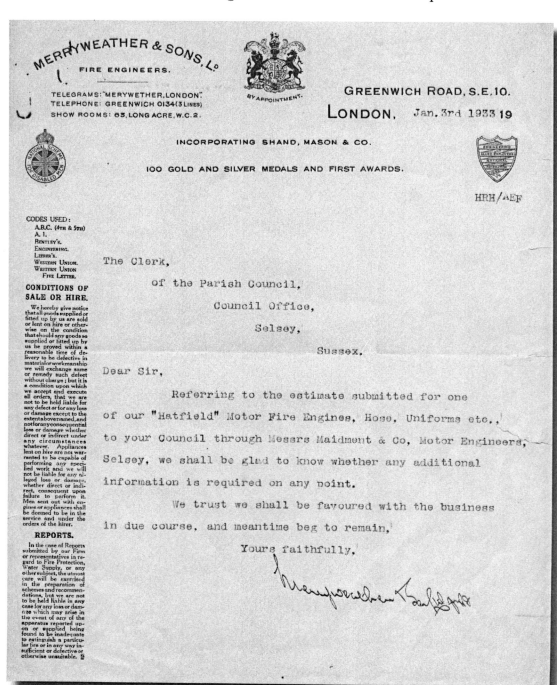

While these enquiries were taking place, there was discontent at the Parish Council, as indicated by the minutes of the Special Parish Meeting held on 13th December 1932:

> *Owing to the unavoidable absence of the Chairman, Mr Day, it was proposed by Mr Hopkins, seconded by Mr Selsby, that Mr S B Arnell be elected Chairman. Carried.*
>
> *The notice convening the meeting was read. The minutes of the meeting held on Monday, 27 June 1932 were read, confirmed and signed. Under "matters arising from the minutes", Mr White raised an objection to the correction of the last amendment which he proposed, which was carried, in that they should not proceed with the purchase of the fire engine until they knew if they could obtain a loan and at what price. This was not included in the minutes and the minutes were therefore wrong, claimed Mr White.*
>
> *The Chairman put the following to the meeting for a vote: whether the minute should be altered or not. 15 voted against it being altered and 5 in favour.*
>
> *The Chairman then read the letter received from WSCC and it was proposed by Mr White that a motor fire engine be bought at a cost not exceeding £500. As there was no-one to second the motion, it was not carried.*
>
> *Mr Hopkins, Chairman of the Fire Committee, explained the cost of the engine and equipment adding that a 1¼d rate for fifteen years would cover the cost. The Chairman confirmed that the Fire Brigade had offered to keep the machine in order and that Mr Maidment had agreed to garage the engine for the exclusive rent of £20 per annum.*
>
> *It was proposed by Mr Hopkins and seconded by Mr Selsby: "that the consent of the meeting be given to the incurring by the Parish Council of an expenditure of £1,000 for the provision of a motor fire engine and equipment for the Parish of Selsey." There were 45 votes in favour and 1 against, inevitably Mr White.*
>
> *Mr Arnell explained very fully the great necessity of a motor fire engine for Selsey. He made reference to the many very advantageous terms the WSCC was offering. He resumed his seat amid applause.*

On 5th January 1933 the Minister of Health requested more detail about the loan. At this point a formal request was made to West Sussex County Council, ignoring the offers received from the City of London even though their interest rate was lower.

The Dennis fire engine was brought down to Selsey for a demonstration and in February Dennis Bros Ltd wrote stating that they had been in contact with Mr Maidment regarding the purchase of the fire engine. They assumed that it was unlikely that the Ministry of Health would turn down the request for the loan and were anxious to come to an agreement on the sale of the fire engine. They asked for more definite information about the situation as it stood, since they had been holding this machine and were naturally anxious to get the matter settled.

On 20th March the Council members requested details of other fire engines that had been demonstrated. Apparently they were not aware of the letter from Dennis Bros Ltd which clearly suggested that the 'powers that be' had already decided to buy. Only at this stage was it agreed that the Dennis fire engine should be purchased.

The Dennis Fire Engine

The West Sussex County Council despatched information to the Minister of Health, suggesting that the loan would be for not less than ten years. They also requested some length of hose, since the existing hose was practically unserviceable. They enclosed a photograph of the proposed Dennis fire engine, stating that, in their judgement, this machine was most suitable for their requirements. They also indicated that other types of fire engine had been demonstrated, notably from Ford, Simonis, Morris, Bedford, Leyland and Merryweather. Mr Maidment had agreed that a lockup garage in the centre of the village would be available.

On 9th June 1933 the Minister of Health gave consent to the loan as follows:

> *I am directed by the Minister of Health to refer to your letter of 30th ultimo, and to forward to you herewith formal consent to the borrowing by the Parish Council of Selsey of the sums of £625 and £251 for fire brigade purposes. The former sum is in respect of the purchase of a motor fire engine and the latter sum is made up of £195 for 2,000 feet of hose and £56 for hose cleaner and spares.*

The letter went on to add that the provision of belts, axes, lines and helmets was not a proper subject for loan sanction. This letter was accompanied by a formal document with the official seal of the Minister of Health for the consent of the loan.

In the meantime, the press were still keeping an eye on Selsey and its Fire Brigade.

On 1st July 1933, the 'Bognor Regis Post' reported:

Selsey Billets
That Fire Engine

> *It has happened! Selsey's accepted wits will raise a different sort of laugh now, and this time it will be against them. Selsey's long proposed fire engine has provided them with happy material. So many formalities had to be gone through that it seemed as though Selsey would never have the new fire fighting apparatus for which the Parish Meetings voted. But Selsey is to have that fire engine, in spite of pessimists and humorists, for I have been given to understand on the very best of authority that not only has it been definitely ordered, but that it will be in Selsey within a month from now. Moreover Selsey's firemen have been measured for their new uniforms, and other equipment is on order.*

The new Dennis fire engine with crew
L to R top row: Albert Bishop, Ted Mason, 'Pert' Maidment, Len Clough, Fred Head
L to R middle row: J Harman, Bert Sayers, Ralph Selsby, Bill Head, Lewis Maidment
L to R bottom Row: Spen Johnson, Ted Mitchell

The Dennis fire engine was delivered at the beginning of August and the Fire & Lighting Committee of the Parish Council had already set about disposing of Selsey's redundant equipment. Having contacted East Wittering Parish Council offering them the old equipment for the sum of £20, they received the following reply on 12th July 1933:

Dear Sir,

Your offer of fire appliances was considered by the Parish Council last evening and a deputation was appointed to inspect the appliances with a view to purchase.
Will you kindly let me know when and where the appliances may be seen.

Yours faithfully,
A J Nixon (Clerk)

Subsequently an offer of £15 was made after the inspection and on 11th October the following letter was sent by East Wittering Parish Council:

Dear Sir,

On August 9th I wrote on behalf of the above Council offering £15 for your disused Fire Fighting Appliances, but have received no reply. The Council would be glad to know if you have come to a decision on the matter.

Yours faithfully,
A J Nixon (Clerk)

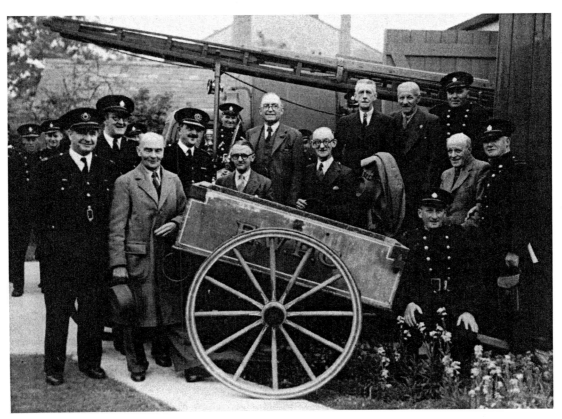

The Croydon/Selsey handcart in East Wittering Livery.
The picture was taken during the 1940s

Meanwhile Selsey Parish Council had agreed to accept the offer of £15 on 9th October and East Wittering responded immediately:

> *I thank you for your letter re Fire Appliances. I will arrange for a meeting of the Council as soon as possible to decide on a place where the appliances can be kept and will let you know when we can accept delivery.*
>
> *Yours faithfully,*
> *A J Nixon (Clerk)*

The Fire Brigade minutes also contained costs of incidental items which the Ministry of Health would not authorise:

Mr J Faers	belts, axes etc	£22. 9s. 6d
Mr A Kennett	clothing	£57. 5s. 6d
Mr H J Sherrington	boots	£23. 0s. 0d
Messrs Simms	helmets	£26.19s. 6d
Mr Maidment	ins etc	£18.11s. 2½d

The Parish Council decided to press West Sussex County Council to extend the loan to cover these items but the reply from County Hall stated that, after some consideration on their legal position, they regretted that they could not agree to any of the suggested amendments made by the Parish Council.

The Rural District Council meanwhile suggested that, since Selsey was now provided with a proper fire engine, they might consider making arrangements for the use of the same fire engine to be available at fires occurring in the Parish of Sidlesham and that this could be effected by setting up a joint committee.

12 – Payment and Servicing

It wasn't long before there were disputes over repair bills, but there were also opportunities to put the new engine through its paces

Bearing in mind that the demonstration model had been 'kept by' for Selsey for almost a year, it was not surprising that Dennis Bros Ltd now wanted their money. They provided a monthly statement of account, dated 30th September 1933, which indicated that they had received nothing so far in payment of the £659.3s.6d owed to them and on the 18th October a formal request in writing for the outstanding payment was received, 'failing which we shall be glad to have a line from you as to when payment may be expected'.

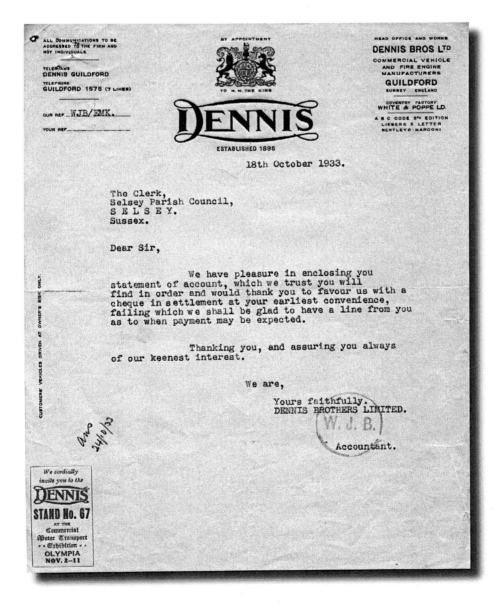

It appears that final documents agreeing to the loan by the County Council were not signed and returned until the end of October, when at last a cheque for £876 was sent to Selsey Parish Council.

WEST SUSSEX COUNTY COUNCIL.

TELEPHONE NOS. 24 & 25.
FW/G
COUNTY TREASURER.
M. T. HUGHES, A.S.A.A.

COUNTY TREASURER'S OFFICE,
CHICHESTER.

IN REPLY PLEASE QUOTE:- 28 October, 1933.

Dear Sir,

Loan for Fire Engine

I enclose cheque dated 1st November, 1933, amounting to £876 for the loan in this case. I will shortly forward an account for the cost of stamp duty, etc.

Yours faithfully,

M. T. Hughes
County Treasurer.

The Clerk,
Selsey Parish Council,
Selsey.

Along with the new fire engine, the members of the Brigade were insured by the London and Lancashire Insurance Company. The list of members on the schedule was as follows:

R Selsby (Captain)	T S Johnson	J Harman
L Maidment Junr (Vice-Captain)	W Head	A Bishop
P Maidment	F Head	E Mitchell
A Sayers	L Clough	E Mason

The annual premium for these men was £5.5s.0d. This is the equivalent of 43.5p per year, per man. Nowadays this would appear to be the bargain of the year!

It was agreed that the Brigade hold fortnightly practices during the winter. The Fire Committee were further empowered to arrange any adjustment and replacement to the fire engine in accordance with the guarantee referred to in the original quotation from Dennis Bros Ltd. Future correspondence was to be sent through the proper channel. (It appears that Mr Maidment had been the main correspondent so far.)

A serious rick fire at Fish Shops Farm in November 1933 gave the Brigade the opportunity to demonstrate their new engine to the village. An unattributed newspaper article reveals[30]:

Selsey Rick Fire Alarm
House and Farm Buildings Threatened

Firemen's Long Fight into the Early Hours
Horses and Cattle Saved

A fierce blaze, attributed to a carelessly flung firework, which destroyed three 40-ton hay ricks and three straw ricks late on Saturday night, threatened to involve a number of houses and farm buildings in the East Road district of Selsey.

The ricks, valued, with farm implements destroyed, at several hundreds of pounds, were owned by Messrs. Selsby and Co., of Fishshops Farm.

---

[30] This is a transcript from a newspaper cutting belonging to Philip Bishop, son of Fireman Bert Bishop.

Fish Shops Farm

The recently-formed Selsey Fire Brigade, under Chief Officer Selsby and Second Officer Maidment made a smart turn-out with the new Dennis engine in response to an alarm given at 11 p.m. by a Mr Pennycord, of Albion-road, Selsey.

On arrival, the ricks were found to be well alight, and efforts were concentrated on the adjacent farm buildings. A sharp breeze fanned the flames along the walls of a 200ft. barn.

With assistance from Police-Sergeants Dabson, Morris and PC Osman and members of the public, 81 pigs and a number of horses and cattle were released from the buildings and driven into the fields.

For three and a half hours the Brigade fought strenuously, with several lines of hose, concentrating on a row of nine houses, one of which was thatch roofed. Barns which were a few feet from the blazing ricks could only be approached by firemen wearing gas masks. The heat from the flames which were visible far out to sea was intense.

Danger Overcome

In the early hours of the morning, all danger to surrounding property was overcome, although a guard was maintained throughout the night and yesterday on the smouldering remnants of the ricks.

In the presence of a crowd of four or five hundred, the Brigade performed its first baptism of flame with honours.

Described by a police officer as 'one of the most dangerous propositions seen in the district for many years', the members of the Brigade drew loud praise for their expert effort. An officer of a Metropolitan Brigade, who was an onlooker, remarked that as a first performance in dealing with such a large outbreak, the training received must have been extremely creditable.

Owing to all night duty, the Brigade were unable to attend the Armistice service yesterday morning at the Parish Church. Much labour had been expended to ensure a smart turn-out, but the Brigade in action has now established a higher reputation than could be gained on parade.

It is understood that the damage is covered by insurance.

A lesser known and possibly more interesting fact was that 'such was the speed at which the crew turned out that two arrived without their false teeth. This was not a serious problem until it came to eating their bread and cheese which they were quite unable to manage.'

On 28th February 1934, a damaging fire broke out at the Golf Club, which was reported in a number of papers. On 7th March 1934, the 'Observer & West Sussex Recorder' reported:

The Golf Club Fire

The outstanding feature of interest in Selsey last week was the fire at the Golf House. The Fire Brigade were called out at about 10 o'clock and were soon on the scene. The fire spread so quickly however, that by the time of their arrival it was impossible to save the building and contents, including golf bags, clubs, bottles of spirits and wine. It is thought that flames in the chimney caught the woodwork.

The Golf Club in 1914

The 'South of England Advertiser' gave this account on 8th March 1934:

Golf Club House Fire

A bad fire occurred at the Golf Club house last week, and the main building was gutted. The cause of the outbreak is not known. An alarm was received by Selsey Fire Brigade just before 10 am, and, although the brigade were on the scene in six minutes, the fire had gained a strong hold, and they could not save the building. Water was pumped for over two hours from a rife near. The house was in a more or less isolated spot, and owing to the fire having made telephonic communication impossible, some delay was apparently caused in giving the alarm.

…and on Saturday 10th March 1934, the 'Hampshire Telegraph and Post' had this to say:

Bouquet for the Fire Brigade

Mr Keep[31] asked if he might throw just a 'little bouquet' at the Fire Brigade, referring to the fire at the Golf Club last week. The way the Brigade came up to the Golf Club was simply splendid.

---

[31] Mr G F Keep was one of the directors of the Golf Club. He lived in Norton Lea.

He wished it recorded in the Minutes that he passed a hearty vote of thanks to the Brigade for the good work done.

The comment found in Mr Ted Mason's book of reports[32] was:

A proper fire this time. A very good turn-out but so it ought to have been, seeing that several members knew that the place had been burning for at least a quarter of an hour before the call was received...

Unfortunately could not rescue any beer, the bottles blowing up like bombs. The Secretary, however, weighed in OK at the Crown on return.

An invoice from Dennis Bros Ltd, dated 29th June 1934, gives an interesting insight into the cost of repairing the fire engine:

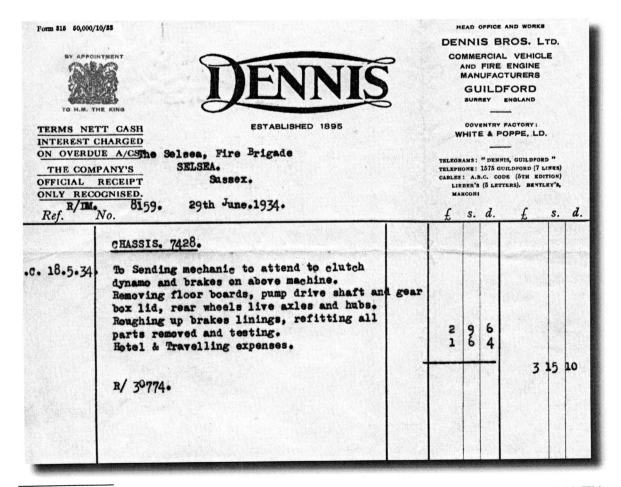

---

[32] Mr Ted Mason, one of the firemen and a member of the Golf Club, kept a book of reports from 1934. This was mentioned in a newspaper article printed in January 1962.

This account was challenged and on the following day a cancellation of the invoice was received. The repair had failed to meet approval as indicated by this letter from Dennis Bros Ltd:

> *16th August 1934*
>
> *Dear Sir,*
>
> *Further to our letter of 9th instant, in connection with the clutch slipping and the attention required to the brakes and battery on the Selsey Fire Engine, we shall be pleased if you can conveniently arrange to let us have this vehicle back as we feel it would be to our mutual advantage if the necessary adjustments were carried out at these Works.*
>
> *If you cannot conveniently arrange to bring the machine back, we will, if given a date, arrange to collect same.*

Even this cooperation from Dennis Bros did not solve the problem as is shown by a further letter from Dennis Bros on 19th September 1934 from the Service Manager:

> *Dear Sir,*
>
> *We are in receipt of your letter of the 16th instant, and regret to note that the Fire Engine which was recently returned to us is reported to be not to your satisfaction as regards the brakes and dynamo.*
>
> *On looking through our records we find that the knock that was reported in the dynamo when received at these Works was due to same having been fitted with a belt with various thicknesses of links. When the correct type of belt was fitted the knock entirely disappeared and we feel sure there is no mechanical defect in the dynamo and that it left here in good condition.*
>
> *As regards the brakes, these were inspected and adjusted and we obtained standard braking efficiency for this type of machine considering the use, etc., it has had. It is possible, of course, to even improve on the brakes possibly by fitting new brake linings but we did not consider that you would wish to go to this expense to obtain this extra braking efficiency.*

We consider that the attention that was given to the vehicle on this last occasion by us should have met with your entire satisfaction and we shall be pleased to have your further comments.

The Parish Clerk replied acknowledging that a new belt was being fitted to the dynamo and confirming that they hoped the slight knock would disappear but he continued:

With regards to the braking system we are quite prepared to accept your statement that standard efficiency was obtained in your test. We cannot at present go to the expense of fitting new linings and trust we shall have no trouble with this part of the machine.

In the midst of the disagreement over the mechanical shortcomings of the new fire engine, it was still required to demonstrate its prowess.

In the August of 1934 there were two fires in two days: The Shack, East Beach on Tuesday 21st and Maidment's Garage on Wednesday 22nd. The 'Chichester Post' of 25th August sets the scene for these fires as follows:

Two fires, one of them the most disastrous which has taken place in Selsey for many years, and a call on the services of the Selsey Lifeboat, provided spectacle and thrills for residents and visitors of Selsey on Tuesday, and in the early hours of Wednesday morning.

On Friday 24th August 1934, the 'Hampshire Telegraph and Post' reported 'The Shack' bungalow fire:

A Bungalow Fire at Selsey
Life-Boat Signal Rockets

Selsey Vessel Out

Yacht Ashore; Then a Bungalow Fire.

Signal rockets were fired about 4 pm on Tuesday summoning the crew of the Selsey Lifeboat to go to the rescue of a small sailing yacht,[33] which had capsized off Wittering.

Under Coxswain Fred Barnes, the lifeboat was quickly launched and on arriving at the Witterings it was ascertained that one of the occupants of the yacht had swum ashore to get help,[34] leaving two others clinging to the bottom of the overturned yacht.

---

[33] Belonging to the Itchenor Sailing Club.
[34] Being helped ashore by London Girl Guides who were at camp in the district.

Fortunately the wind and tide were favourable, and the yacht drifted aground, so that the services of the lifeboatmen were not required.

The life-boat then returned to Selsey and on the way back picked up an empty dinghy, which had apparently slipped its moorings, and towed it home to Selsey.

Thatched Roof Ablaze

Immediately after the Signal rockets had been fired from ground adjoining to summon the lifeboat crew, it was discovered that the thatched roof of a bungalow, named the Shack, situated in Coastguard Lane,[35] was on fire. There was a terrific wind, and the roof speedily became a blazing mass.

The Shack bungalow fire.
Left to right are Ralph Selsby, Bill Head, Ted Mitchell and Spen Johnson

The bungalow was the joint property of Mr Malcolm McNeille, the Chichester photographer, and Dr. Serjeant, of Hounslow. The doctor had been in residence there during August, but on Tuesday afternoon was in Chichester, with the other occupants,[36] and the only living things in the bungalow were a couple of dogs, one of which – a favourite Pekingese – lost its life.

---

[35] Coastguard Lane is now in the sea but ran in a similar position to Kingsway.
[36] His wife and young daughter and a nephew. An alternative spelling of 'Sargent' is also used.

> *The fire alarm was sounded and a very smart turn out quickly brought the Selsey Fire Brigade on the scene.*[37]
>
> *The fire brigade, assisted by the police, were able to save most of the personal property of the doctor, but the fire had such a hold that the bungalow itself, together with the furniture, was practically burnt out. The bungalow was insured, but not the furniture.*

This fire was also reported in the 'Daily Mail', the 'West Sussex Gazette', and the 'Chichester Post'.

The 'Daily Mail' and the 'Chichester Post' both express the opinion that it was the rocket which was fired to bring the lifeboat crew to their stations which started the fire at The Shack. The Royal National Lifeboat Association is unable to confirm whether or not this was so.

Six months later, on 21st February 1935, there was a letter from Summers, Henderson & Co. to Selsey Parish Council:

> *re The Shack, Fishing Beach, Coastguards Lane, Selsey*
>
> *We thank you for your letter of the 15th inst., in connection with the above, and have to again inform you that our Principals have no further interest in the matter.*
>
> *We would mention that, as we understand the position, the bungalow was in dual ownership of Dr. Serjeant, and Mr. Malcolm McNeille, 26, South Street, Chichester, and we think these two gentlemen should be held responsible for the outstanding payment of £3.7.7.*

A handwritten note states that both parties were written to on 25th February 1935 requesting an early remittance.

The 'Chichester Post' of 25th August 1934 had this report on the fire at Maidment's garage:

> *The second fire, which was discovered shortly after two o'clock on Wednesday morning, caused damage amounting to thousands of pounds, and only the heroic efforts of the Selsey Fire Brigade assisted by helpers and a troop of London Scouts, under canvas at Medmerry, prevented the garage owned by Mr L Maidment from being involved.*

---

[37] The exact time was recorded as 4.16 and the brigade was away in one and a half minutes. The firemen were unable to leave the scene until 7.54

The Sleepers Awake!

The building involved in the second fire were premises at the back of the Pavilion tenanted by Mr P Gray, a Selsey carrier who lives in East Road, and owned by Mrs E Gardener, of Lewes Road [sic]. The upper floor was filled with furniture, while on the ground floor there was a large lorry, and it is believed, two other motor vehicles. In the same yard is a stable owned by Mr P Jones, of the Premier Riding School, and only a low wall separates it from the large garage owned by Mr L Maidment, where the Selsey Fire-engine is housed.

The outbreak was discovered by two young men, who, unable to find lodging, had been given permission to sleep in a car in Maidment's Garage. They were awakened by choking clouds of smoke, and they immediately gave the alarm. The fire hooter was sounded at about twenty minutes to two, and the Brigade, under chief Officer R Selsby and Second Officer L M Maidment, were on the scene of the outbreak three minutes later, and were playing water on the flames within five minutes of receiving the call.

Bert Bishop & fire engine outside Maidment's workshop

Between 60 and 70 cars were in the garage at the time and these were quickly wheeled out, as the structure, which is timber build, was in great danger.

In an extraordinarily short space of time, High Street and East Road was packed with people, residents in houses in the immediate neighbourhood who were awakened by the dense volumes of smoke which rolled in through their bedroom windows, rising in the belief that their own homes were on fire.

When the fire brigade arrived on the scene it was immediately obvious that nothing could be done to save Mr Gray's premises. The building was a mass of flames, and the corrugated iron doors were red hot.

The brigade concentrated their efforts on confining the blaze to the store and preventing it spreading to the garage and the stables. There were five horses in the stables, and[38] these were led out by Mr Bob Pratt who was helped by other people and a troop of London Scouts who worked heroically, one of them[39] badly cutting his hand in smashing the window of the stables. Afterwards, they took their position on the roof of the garage, and with buckets of water, doused the sparks, which, blown by the high wind, threatened the garage buildings.

The floor and the roof of the store, collapsed in a shower of sparks, and the brigade played their hose on it for several hours, eventually leaving the scene of the outbreak at 7.30, although it was got under control within half an hour.

Only the blackened walls are now standing. Inside is an indistinguishable heap of ashes and charred wood, the only identifiable articles being the burned chassis of a large lorry, a tin trunk, a picture and pails and buckets.[40]

Great credit is due to the brigade for the magnificent way in which they worked, and the members of the brigade are themselves loud in their praise of the London Scouts for the splendid manner in which they helped. At one time Mr Maidment was fully convinced that nothing could save his premises. The origin of the fire is a mystery.

---

[38] After the stable doors had been prised open with poles – according to the 'Hampshire Telegraph & Post'
[39] Named in another report as RSM Bland, of the St Clement's Troop, Barnesbury
[40] A report in the 'West Sussex Gazette' states that Mr Gray also lost two cars, a van and a quantity of furniture.

The 'West Sussex Gazette' of 23rd August 1934 reported:

It is understood that in the case of both fires the damage is only partly covered by Insurance. Police from Chichester, including Sergts. Dabson and Morris and several constables also helped the firemen.

On 29th August 1934 the 'Observer & West Sussex Recorder' had this comment to make regarding the two fires:

Editorial
The Fire Engine

Once upon a time, in a growing district on the East Coast, the legend existed that no one ever died there. And for many years there was truth in it – and the reason? Because there was nowhere in which to lay them to sleep. Churchyards were full and could no longer be used except by those who already owned family vaults, and as mortality was practically non-existent, there was no immediate haste necessary in making other provisions. The wee township had won fame – the healthiest spot in England. Then arose a town council – most energetic because newborn. A cemetery must be provided. So land was acquired adjoining a peaceful road in the suburbs. This was bounded by stone coping and high iron railing. All was ready. The gates were thrown open and sad little processions entered. The spell was broken. So was the ground, by many a new-made mound. The happenings in Selsey during this week reminded us of the above true tale. There were no fire-fighting appliances (worthy of the name). The place was growing out of all recognition. A fire engine must be provided – and it was so. Excellent and much-needed. But in twenty-four hours there were two big blazes, one in the heart of the village, a store used for warehousing furniture having completely burned out, the other a bungalow on the east beach, which also left no salvage. Because provision has been made, must the fire fiend come amongst us?

It should be remembered that it was the chrome plated demonstration model that was purchased and perhaps the mechanical problems were the result of its previous use prior to coming to Selsey. In the middle of December 1934, Dennis Bros Ltd wrote once again as follows:

We regret to note that the braking system is not to your satisfaction. No doubt you will recall that when we last had this vehicle in it was considered that an improvement could be made by replacing the liners, etc., but you could not see your way clear at that time to advise us to carry out the work.

We shall be pleased to attend to the brakes on this machine if you can arrange to let us have it. We regret to say, however, that we have not a replacement that we can loan you in the event of your so doing. Possibly you could make arrangements locally.

Any time would be convenient for us to have the vehicle and we look forward to hearing from you. We would remind you, however, that we are closing down for the Christmas holiday from 22nd to 27th instant.

Fortunately the fire engine was still in Selsey when it appears that there was a fire at Pennicott's, in the High Street, at the end of 1934. It is surprising that this fire was not reported in the paper. In its heyday Pennicott's sold millinery, dress fabric, haberdashery and ready-to-wear garments, and upstairs there was a gentlemen's tailor. It existed until the 1970s and was situated where Penny Lane is today.

High St looking north towards Pennicott's

The only indication of this fire is a letter of 21st January 1935 from Draper's & General Insurance Company Ltd stating:

Fire at Pennicott's Drapery Store Policy DLBX.7034.

We duly received your letter of the 4th. Inst. And have been making inquiries regarding the Insurer's of the building concerned. This, we find, is insured through the Westminster Fire Office and we are in communication with them regarding the apportionment of the Fire Brigade account.

On receipt of their reply, we will advise you.

The machine was ultimately taken to the Works in January 1935 and the following invoice was received in May 1935:

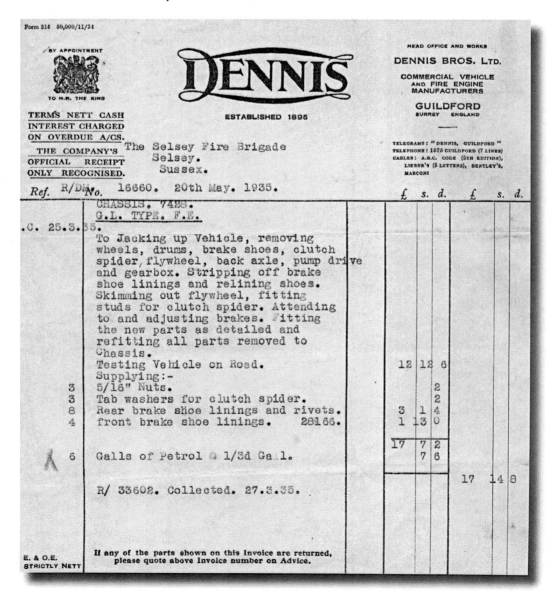

While this was being discussed Mr Francis read the report of the Fire and Lighting Committee commenting on the excellent and enthusiastic way the Fire Brigade were carrying out their duties, but the Committee had inspected the Fire Station (garage) and found uniforms and equipment were covered with mildew caused by damp. Action was taken in having the Fire Station match boarded at a cost of £4.16s.

The enthusiasm of the firemen was demonstrated at a rather different type of fire, which was reported on Wednesday 5th June 1935 in the 'Observer & West Sussex Recorder':

Motor-Cycle in Flames

A motor-cycle in flames on the old tramway bridge,[41] early on Thursday afternoon, provided the village with a brief thrill. The motor-cyclist who comes from Brighton, was riding into Selsey, when he noticed flames coming from his rather antiquated machine. The Fire Brigade made a smart turn out and under Chief Officer R Selsby the fire was soon subdued.

…followed by an interesting entry in the Parish Council Minutes dated 8th July 1935:

Mrs L Gardener revealed that the Council were experiencing difficulty obtaining a sum of just £5, the expenses charged by the Fire Brigade for extinguishing a motor cycle fire which occurred just near the Bridge. The rider was not on his own machine, and the insurance company of the owner 'are not interested'. So the Clerk of the Council sought advice from the National Fire Brigade Association. They advised settlement should be made by the rider, failing that he should be sued in the County Court.

Slight doubt was cast as to whether the judge would allow for the services of eleven firemen, as it seems an excessive number of men to put out one motor cycle fire.

In April the Fire Brigade had been given permission to take part in the Silver Jubilee celebrations for King George V, which probably indicates that the repairs had been satisfactorily carried out, but the account with Dennis Bros Ltd still caused concern:

---

[41] This is the 'bridge' which is by the former police houses in Chichester Road. An ornamental pond belonging to Bunn Leisure can be seen on the right hand side, coming into Selsey.

> *In reply to your letter of the 2nd instant, in connection with charges made on Invoice R/DM.16660, we cannot understand why you suggest that your Council cannot see why they should be responsible for this payment. May we respectfully point out to you our letter of 19th September wherein we advised you to further improve the brakes it would be necessary to reline same and as we thought you would not go to that expense we did not line them on that particular occasion.*
>
> *Further, in our letter of 18th December we again pointed out that it would be necessary to receive your instructions before we could fit the brake linings referred to. Therefore, when we received your instructions to do so, we were under the impression, of course, that by asking us to do this you had agreed to meet the cost of the brake linings.*
>
> *We trust, therefore, when the matter has been reconsidered you will see your way clear to meet the account as rendered.*

However in September the amount was still under dispute and a deputation was despatched to Guildford to attempt to resolve the issue. On 18th November 1935 a note arrived from Dennis Bros Ltd:

> *On going through our book we find that the account May 20th - £17.14s.8d. in respect of repairs carried out to your Fire Engine, is still outstanding.*
>
> *This now being somewhat overdue, we shall be glad if you will let us know when we may expect payment.*
>
> *Thanking you in advance …*

On 25th February 1936 the debt was still outstanding and produced the following diplomatic and imaginatively phrased letter:

> *Our Accounts Dept., has called my attention to the outstanding balance of £17.14s.8d. which we have on our books, as a result of some work done on your Motor Fire Engine.*
>
> *On looking back over the correspondence, the writer finds that a letter from Mr Frank Keep asked us not to press this account, as he and Mr Francis would probably be coming up to talk the matter over. The proposed visit was to have taken place in October of last year.*

> *Apparently, since then nothing else has transpired and the visit did not mature.*
>
> *The writer is really very anxious indeed to get this job squared up, and it would really appear that the sum which we have on our books is eligible for payment on your part, and we hope you will drop us a line on the subject. On the other hand, would you care for us to take the job up direct with Mr Keep, who is of course, very well known to us personally?*
>
> *As far as the writer is concerned all he wants is to get the job settled one way or the other, and trusts you will favour us with a reply to this letter.*

Although not minuted, further contacts must have been made and a deputation finally visited the works. On 5th March 1936 the following letter was received:

> *Dear Sir,*
>
> *With further reference to your visit to these Works yesterday afternoon together with your colleague regarding the charges made on Invoice R/DM.16660 dated 20th May 1935, we think the question was carefully gone into as regards the payment of this invoice, and in view of the suggestions made, the matter has been placed before Mr Downing for consideration.*
>
> *In order to assist you, purely as an ex gratia offer, in this instance, we are prepared to accept £10.0.0. in cancellation of this invoice.*
>
> *We should be pleased to hear that in view of this generous offer it will enable you to have the account passed for payment, and we should thank you for your confirmation of same, on receipt of which a Credit Note will be put through accordingly.*
>
> *Assuring you of our co-operation at all times…*

Surprisingly, this offer did not meet with approval and the matter was referred back to the Fire Committee with the requirement that the details of the guarantee and the accounts from Dennis Bros Ltd be produced.

In July it was agreed that another deputation of two members visit the Dennis works and that they be empowered to treat and settle with Dennis Bros Ltd.

In October the Committee accepted the recommendations of the deputation and agreed to settle the account of £10 – after a lapse of one and a half years and several deputations, all for less than £8!

13 – Fires and More Fires

– but at least the Brigade have the right equipment to deal with them

The years 1937 and 1938 were rather prolific ones for fires, and Fire Brigade matters were mainly dealt with by the Fire Brigade Committee (see chapter 14). Although not all of the fires appear to have been reported in the press, this chapter reports the information we have.

On 19th January 1937 there was a fire at 'The Homestead'[42] in the High Street (to the left of Lloyds Bank), reported in the 'Chichester Observer' on 27th January:

Empty House Ablaze
£500 Damage at Selsey

Between £500 and £600 worth of damage was done when a fire broke out in the roof of the Homestead, High Street, Selsey, on Tuesday evening of last week.

The house was under repair and no-one was living there at the time, the house being the property of Mr. Heron Allen.

The Homestead

---

[42] Among the Homestead's various incarnations, it has been a doctor's house, a dentist's house and surgery and a bed and breakfast.

Mrs Swindells, a neighbour, said that she was going out of the back door of her house when she saw that the roof of the Homestead was in flames. She immediately ran out and phoned the fire station. The fire brigade had some difficulty in putting out the fire, and did not leave until about 11 pm.

On 30th January 1937, the 'Chichester Post' had this to say:

Serious Roof Fire

The Selsey Fire Brigade recently stopped what would have been a serious fire when they received a call to the Homestead, belonging to Mr E Heron-Allen, of Large Acres, Selsey. The Brigade received a call at 7 pm, they found the thatch of the Homestead, which has been completely renovated, and was still in the hands of the builders, well alight. The fire was breaking through the thatch which, at that point, was five feet thick.

Considerably hampered by the fact that it was covered with wire netting, the Brigade, under Chief Officer Selsby, ran one hose inside the house, and directed another on to the roof from outside, while firemen stripped part of the roof. They soon had the fire under control, and stood by until midnight, but there was no further outbreak. Fortunately, there was little or no wind; had there been, the fire would have assumed dangerous proportions, for on one side there is Mr Swindell's estate office, and nearby a bank and a garage.

Less than two weeks later, on Sunday 31st January, there was another fire, this time at the Petersfield and Selsey Gas Offices, at the southern end of the High Street, now Den's Fish Bar next door to Clarkson's Off Licence.

It is rather surprising that such an important fire should go unreported but perhaps this is explained by the fact that the fire took place on a Sunday. Mrs Hazel Ousley (née Rose) remembers the fire as her father, Mr Walter Clement Rose, was the Manager at the time and he and his family lived in the accommodation behind and over the offices. The house went with the job.

Above the offices, there was a large room with a fireplace at each end and one of these fireplaces was the cause of the fire. A wooden beam caught fire. As the Fire Brigade commented at the time that the beam was 'wrongly situated' it is likely that it ran under the fireplace and was set alight by the heat of the fire upstairs. Mrs Ousley's brother (Tony Rose) was a baby in a cot in the room next door and this room was full of smoke. The children were very frightened.

Clem Rose in his office

A letter from the Westminster Fire Office, dated 6th May 1937, stated:

> *Fire at Petersfield and Selsey Gas Offices. Policy no. 1113038*
>
> *With further reference to our letter of 30th April, we have now received our Assessors' report on the extinction expenses in connection with this fire. We have pleasure in enclosing our cheque for £7.11s.8d. and shall be obliged by your acknowledgement in due course.*
>
> *A remittance for the balance of 12s.4d. should reach you from the Brighton Branch of the Royal Exchange Assurance simultaneously with this letter.*

… and (as promised) also on 6th May 1937 there was a letter from the Royal Exchange Assurance to Selsey Parish Council:

> *re Fire at Offices of Petersfield & Selsey Gas Co., High Street, Selsey. 31st January 1937.*
>
> *We enclose herewith cheque for 12/4d. being our proportion of the Fire Brigade expenses for services rendered at an outbreak of fire at the above premises, and we shall be pleased to receive an acknowledgement of this amount at your earliest convenience.*

In early August 1937 there was a fire at the back of The Fun Palace in the High Street. The Fun Palace was the rather dilapidated hut, most recently a second-hand shop, opposite the Fire Station. It contained slot machines. Anecdotal evidence indicates that the results of this fire remained visible in the roof space until its demolition in the autumn of 2007.

The 'Fun Palace' building before being demolished in the autumn of 2007

On Saturday, 21st August 1937 'The Post' reported:

Fire at Amusement Palace

Few local residents realise what a narrow escape the Fun Palace in the High Street had from being destroyed by fire last Saturday week.

At 12.30 pm the Fire Brigade was called to a fire at an outhouse behind the palace, and headed by Chief Officer Selsby, they were on the scene.

Despite the brigade's strenuous efforts, the outhouse was completely destroyed and for some time it was touch and go whether or not the flames would spread to the main building.

As it was, it was found sufficient to wrench several smouldering boards from the back of the palace, which is an entirely wooden structure. Had the flames obtained any hold on the building it would have been burned to the ground in a very short time. The Brigade left the scene at 3 am – two and a half hours after their arrival.

A letter from Sun Insurance Office Ltd, dated 15th September 1937, contained payment for the Fire Brigade's services:

> *8 August 1937 Fire at the Fun Palace, High Street, Selsey*
>
> *Policy no. F/.16625008.*
>
> *We enclose cheque for £10.9.6. in settlement of our proportion of the Fire Brigade Account rendered in connection with the above.*

There was a gap of over nine months until the next fire. On Thursday 12th May 1938 a fire at the Off Licence at the southern end of the High Street (almost opposite West Street) could have been a lot worse. The Off Licence is now Clarksons. This report was in the 'West Sussex Gazette' of 19th May:

> *The Fire Brigade was called out about 9 pm on Thursday to the off-licence premises in Hillfield-road. Though it was only a chimney fire, it was 'terrifying' states an eye-witness, and even the firemen admit it was the worst of its kind that they had ever had to tackle. The thatch caught alight, and it was but a question of seconds whether the outbreak could be got under control or would demolish the whole structure. The customary promptitude of the brigade saved the situation.*

The Off Licence today

The Brigade sought to claim the usual charges, and Selsey Parish Council received a letter from the Atlas Assurance Company Limited on 26th May stating:

> *re Fire at Off Licence, High Street, Selsey. 12th May 1938*
>
> *Your account in respect of the Brigade charges in this connection has been forwarded to us, but in respect of the charge for the Deputy Officer, should not this Item be included in that for the firemen. Furthermore, kindly advise us how many men other than the Officer in charge attended the fire.*
>
> *In your reply we should be glad if you would kindly bear in mind that the fee under the scale of the national Fire Brigade Association, is limited to one Officer and 12 men.*

On 5th July a further letter from the Atlas Assurance Company Limited informed Selsey Parish Council that:

> *Re Fire at Off Licence, High Street, Selsey*
>
> *We are in receipt of your postcard of the 2nd instant, and would advise you that we have again requested our Inspector to call in connection with this account, and we are asking if he will kindly give this matter his immediate attention.*

This letter from the Atlas Assurance Company Limited, dated 3rd August 1938, shows that the claim was considered to be too high:

> *Re Fire at Off Licence, High Street, Selsey*
>
> *With further reference to the above, we regret to advise you that we are of the opinion that it was not necessary for the whole of the Fire Brigade to spend 2½ hours at the fire, and we feel that half the time charged for is the most that we can be reasonably expected to pay for.*
>
> *We are therefore enclosing herewith a cheque for £5.5.3d. being half the figure at which the account was originally adjusted.*
>
> *We would mention that your acknowledgment on the back of the draft will be sufficient discharge.*

The Parish Council were not happy with this and so sought advice - as can be seen from this reply of the 13th August 1938, from the National Fire Brigades' Association to Mr Harman, Fire Station, Selsey:

> *I am in receipt of your letter of the 10th instant, and I assume that the fire in question occurred within the parish limits, if such is the case, then no legal charge can be made for the services of the Brigade.*
>
> *If on the other hand, the fire occurred outside the limits of the Parish, there is no statutory power which permits a Parish to send its Fire Engine beyond its boundaries, and it is extremely doubtful whether the Parish can recover fees for use of the appliances.*
>
> *Possibly your account only concerns the fees for personnel, and therefore it would seem to be the obvious duty of the Parish Council to pay the men for their services with in the Parish.*
>
> *Insurance Companies cannot be held liable and the offer made to you is ex-gratia, and I think you should accept same, and request the Parish Council to pay the balance of remuneration for the mens time.*

This prompted the Parish Council to send another letter to the Atlas Assurance Company Limited, bringing a swift reply on 7th September:

> *re Fire at Off Licence, High St. Selsey*
>
> *We thank you for your letter of the 5th instant, and observe your remarks.*
>
> *We shall await your further advices after placing the matter before your Finance Committee, but in the meantime would mention that we have paid half the amount of £10.10.6d. consequent upon the adjustment of your account by including the deputy officer as an ordinary fireman.*
>
> *You will no doubt recollect when our Representative saw you in June last you stated that you were content to leave the matter **entirely to us**.*

Finally, on 17th September, the Parish Council received the letter from the Atlas Assurance Company Limited that they were hoping for:

re Fire at Off Licence, High Street, Selsey

With reference to our correspondence in connection with the Selsey Fire Brigade account, this matter has received further consideration, and we have now decided to meet your account in full. Having already forwarded you a cheque for £5.5s.3d, we are enclosing a further one for the balance of £5.19s.9d and your acknowledgement on the back thereof will be sufficient discharge.

We would also ask you if you would please present our cheque sent you on the 3rd ult. for payment in order to discharge the same.

On 14th July 1938 there was a fire at the Fish Shop, in East Street . This shop was owned and run by Miss Hilda Petts. It was opposite East St car park entrance, on the corner of Croft Road.

No press report has been found, but for some reason claims were made to two companies and on 15th August 1938 there are two letters to Selsey Parish Council containing cheques: one from the Phoenix Assurance Company Limited:

Fire at Fish Shop, East Road, Selsey.

With reference to your account in connection with the above, we enclose our cheque for £6.11.6d being our proportion thereof.

… and the other from the Atlas Assurance Company Limited:

re Fire – Fish Shop, East Road, Selsey. 14th July 1938.

We have pleasure in enclosing cheque value £2.1.–d, in settlement of our proportion of your charges for attendance at the above.

Your signature on the back of our cheque will be sufficient acknowledgement for our records.

There was no reference found in the press to a fire in Orchard Avenue on 18th August 1938, but this rather curious correspondence from the Legal Insurance Company to Selsey Parish Council, relating to Brigade charges, still exists:

On 21st October 1938, there is a letter requesting more information:

> *Fire Brigade Charges. Fire at Orchard Avenue, 18.8.38*
>
> *With reference to your enquiry concerning the account forwarded to us in respect of the turnout of the Selsey Brigade for attendance at Orchard Avenue, we much regret not having communicated with you earlier but we have now received particulars from our Insured and if you will kindly inform us the circumstances under which the Insured is liable for payment of the account we shall be pleased to give the matter our further consideration.*

The next letter on 28th November indicates that the Legal Insurance Company is not satisfied with the information they have been given:

> *Brigade Charges. Fire at Orchard Avenue. 18.8.38*
>
> *We are in receipt of your letter of the 24th instant, and note what you write.*
>
> *We assume, however, that the Brigade is 'rate-aided' and if you will let us have information on this point and also a brief account of circumstances under which the call was received and the extent of the damage resulting from the outbreak, also the manner in which our Insured's property was endangered the matter shall receive our further attention.*

The final letter of 2nd December appears to challenge the Brigade's claim for an attendance charge:

> *Brigade Charges. Fire at Orchard Avenue. 18.8.38*
>
> *We note what you write in your letter of the 29th November, and whilst we are prepared to consider contributing towards the account we observe you state that you are not in a position to assess the damage done to the property. You will understand, however, that we are not disposed to agree a payment without particulars of the services which were, in fact, rendered to our Insured and as we have gathered from the latter that he is not aware that any damage was caused we shall be glad if you will kindly arrange for the*

Captain of the Brigade to submit a report, giving details of the place of the outbreak, the damage caused, and all property which was damaged and/or endangered. In the latter respect you will, too, appreciate that if other property in addition to that of our Insured, was threatened the owners or Insurers should be approached to share in the contribution, and information is necessary so that we may take the usual steps.

As there was no further correspondence found, maybe the claim was dropped. This is the last fire we have any records for involving the Selsey Fire Brigade before its transfer to Chichester Rural District Council.

14 – The Fire Brigade Committee

As well as the serious business of firefighting, there is fun and fundraising

[Nothing was known about the Fire Brigade Committee until the Minute Book, owned by Mrs Mollie Phillips, was loaned to the Selsey Society by Mr Christopher Honywood. Later, this Minute Book was donated to the Society when Mrs Phillips moved from Selsey.]

While the Parish Council had its Fire & Lighting Committee, the Fire Brigade had its own Committee consisting of the Chief Officer and all the men.

We speculate that, with the arrival of the Dennis fire engine and the resulting enthusiasm, the Committee was formed with the objective of maintaining that interest after all the ups and downs. In the first minutes, dated August 1933, the last item is Brigade Funds where it was agreed to form a Committee to raise funds for the Brigade. Was it that now they had ceased to chase all over the village pushing a handcart, they had the time and energy to consider social and fundraising activities? It started off well because they agreed that if they received pay for the first three months practice they would donate it to the fund.

The Brigade sought funds to allow them to support the Fire Brigade Widows & Orphans Benevolent Fund and subsequently received a letter thanking them for their donations and asking the Brigade to appoint three members as Life Governors. Chief Officer Selsby and Firemen Harman and Sayers were elected to receive this honour.

The only business recorded at the second meeting was that they should have a boxing tournament in The Pavilion in the first week of December. The quest for subscriptions towards the cost of the prizes clearly set out the pecking order in the village hierarchy: Sir Archibald Hamilton, Mr Edward Heron-Allen, Col. Warren, Mr Bury, Bill Mitchell, Mr Hunnisett, Mr E G Arnell and Mr Heaver.

Mr Marks agreed to be the referee and Mr Francis the Master of Ceremonies. The price of seats was set at 5s.9d and 3s.6d for Ringside seats, 2s.4d for Centre and Balcony seats and 1s.2d for the remainder. These prices seem rather high because very few, if any, people earned £3 per week. The following month entertainment tax was discussed and the question of seat prices reconsidered and changed to 3s.8d, 2s.6d & 1s.6d.

Messrs Marks, Mitchell and Heaver each donated 10s and Mr Hobbs a cup and a medal and 100 posters and 200 programmes were ordered. The tournament was a great success, with the nett profit amounting to £17.17s.3d.

It was not all beer and skittles, however, as within months of the Dennis fire engine arriving the thorny issues of 'cleaning' and 'hose winding' surfaced and they remain a problem to the present day. In the 1940s the activities still appeared to be unpopular and not everyone was doing their share of the work. At both ends of the timescale, they attempted to resolve the problem by organising a rota system – officers were exempt. In December 1935 it was agreed that members who failed to attend would be fined one shilling (the equivalent of two pints of beer).

The Brigade fund was sustained through fundraising, mainly by holding flag days, dances, whist drives and, of course, the boxing match. Their generosity is illustrated by the fact than in 1934 they sent £5 to the Gresford Colliery Disaster Fund and also held a dance in The Pavilion, for which the hire charge was two guineas (£2.2s), in aid of the same good cause.

The AGM in December 1934 was attended by a reporter from the 'Chichester Post' who, at the end of the meeting, was asked to thank the public for the support they had given the Brigade. There was also mention of a 'Challenge Cup', which was on view in the station, (although there is nothing to indicate why it was awarded) and an offer was made by Mr. Spencer (Spen) Johnson, Jeweller and Watchmaker, to display it in his shop window, together with a printed card, and the Secretary was asked to enquire about engraving.

On 20th March the following year, at the Holborn Restaurant, the Chief Officer was presented with the Hammond Cup by Lord Ampthill, on behalf of the Widows & Orphans Benevolent Fund and, at the end of the year, they were also awarded the 'Mant Cup' for the largest collection by a village with a population of under 5000. (The Brigade was awarded this cup again in 1941.) It was agreed that all the cups held by the Brigade should be photographed.

1935 also brought a letter from the British Legion inviting the Brigade to send two representatives to a meeting to consider what steps should be taken to celebrate the King and Queen's Silver Jubilee. The Fire Brigade Committee agreed to give a donation of a guinea and suggested that a fire display should be included in the programme. The demonstration should represent 'Firefighting 25 years ago and the present day' with the proviso that the Jubilee Committee built a dummy house. This proposal was subsequently turned down by the Committee on the grounds of finance.

The Brigade was also invited to take part in a church parade and share the expenses. However, it was later agreed that since the Brigade had already subscribed to the Jubilee Fund they were not in a financial position to make a further donation and owing to several members being on leave they would be unable to make a strong enough muster to take part in the parade.

At the AGM held at end of 1935, it was decided to form an 'Amusement Committee'. Their first task was to organise a dance in the Pavilion in June, where the hire charge had risen sharply since 1934 to £3.10s, and the Casino Five Band was booked for £4. It would seem that this band was all the rage in 1936, as they were also booked for the Annual Charity dance in aid of the Selsey Nursing Association, in October of the same year.

At the following year's AGM there was a complaint that on training nights all they did was inspect hydrants. This and other problems were considered to be so serious that after a lengthy discussion the Secretary was instructed to write to the Chairman of the Fire & Lighting Committee and ask for a joint meeting between that body and the Brigade and request that the Chairman of the Parish Council be invited to attend.

The meeting was held at The Crown on 6th January 1937 with Chief Officer Selsby in the Chair. Attendees consisted of the Fire Brigade, the Chairman of the Parish Council and Lt. Col. Moore, the Chairman of the Fire & Lighting Committee.

The issues of more hydrants, a new siren, a Hose Drying Tower were all to be put before the Council as well as installation of a telephone extension at Mr Maidment's garage for use in the event of night calls. Lt. Col. Moore stated that he was under the impression that this last item had been sanctioned by the Council and he promised to make enquiries about the delay and hurry things up.

Minutes of the Selsey Parish Council give us the following details about the hydrants, the siren and drying tower:

Minute 253 dated 11th January 1937 shows that a tracing plan of hydrants was going to be bought from Selsey Water Company at a cost of 10 shillings.

Minute 255 is dated 24th March 1937 and states that the Finance Committee would be requested to approve the expenditure of £62 for a Hose Drying Tower and £46 for a fire siren.

Minute 260 of 19th April 1937 records that the Fire & Lighting Committee were empowered to deal with the wiring up of the new fire alarm as a matter of urgency and that this wiring would cost up to £15.

It leaves one wondering why these separate items could not all have been discussed at the 11th January meeting rather than being spread over a period of 3 months.

Towards the end of 1937 a meeting was held after the death of second Officer L Maidment and resignation of fireman P Maidment. Chief Officer Selsby proposed the promotion of Third Officer Sayers to Second Officer, Fourth Officer Clough to Third Officer and Fireman Harman to Third Officer. This was seconded by fireman F Head and carried unanimously. The names of Pratt, Rudwick, Phillips, Jerram and Owens were mentioned to fill the two vacancies and it was agreed that Messrs Jerram and Phillips should be appointed.

At the outbreak of WWII, the Auxiliary Fire Service had been formed from volunteers to assist the regular fire brigades. At a meeting held in August 1941 it was explained that the Fire Services Act of 1941 decreed that these two groups would be amalgamated and known as the National Fire Service. The AFS were to be trained in the use of the engine and the regulars in the use of the trailer, so that mixed crews could perform night duty. At this meeting it was also agreed that the Brigade should act as 'Rescue Party' as far as fire duties permitted, in the event of enemy action. However, the Fire Brigade Committee continued to function.

In 1942, the Brigade supported Warship Week by holding a darts tournament which raised £7.8s as a gift to the nation. The prize for the winning team was in the form of saving stamps. It had also been proposed that the Brigade purchase £15 in war bonds but after further consideration the idea was abandoned.

At the same time, it was agreed to spend £2.10s on the purchase of a wireless, with the money to be raised by a special levy of 2s.6d on each member. It was also proposed that as many members as possible attend the Home Guard lectures on the use of firearms.

Throughout the period covered by the Minute Book social activities had been devised by the Brigade Committee but in the final set of minutes, for the twelfth Annual General Meeting in 1948, it was agreed that a General Committee be formed to 'deal with all matters not necessary to put before the full Brigade meeting, or of an emergency nature'. It was also decided that a Social Club be formed by members for the purpose of organising social activities - principally an annual dinner at a fee of five shillings a quarter payable on receipt of the retainer payment. The very last item minuted gives details of a children's party.

15 – The Beginning of the End

Predictably the handover isn't all plain sailing

On 12th January 1939 a letter was received from the Clerk of the Chichester Rural District Council referring to the recent Fire Brigades' Act 1938:

> *I am directed to inform you that it is the intention of the Rural District Council pursuant to the powers conferred by the Fire Brigades' Act to take control of the Selsey Fire Brigade, engine, appliances and equipment as from 29th instant and that they do not propose to delegate their powers under the Act to the (Selsey) Parish Council.*
>
> *I have been authorised to confer with the Chairman of the Parish Council and the Captain of the Brigade on matters arising on the proposal of the District Council, and I shall be glad if you will consult Mr S B Arnell, and let me know when it will be convenient for such conference to take place.*
>
> *Effect will in due course be given to Section 6 of the Act and the financial adjustments to be made consequent on the transfer to the District Council.*

This was the beginning of the end of a fraught relationship between the Parish Council and a fire engine and was the prelude to a series of letters covering the transfer of ownership of the engine and the equipment as well as insurance and the hire of the site.

The people of Selsey weren't all happy with the transfer. On Saturday 11th May 1940, Mr Ralfs, who lived in 'Suntop', York Road, sent the following strongly worded letter to Chichester Rural District Council, with a copy also sent to Selsey Parish Council:

> *re Selsey Fire Brigade*
>
> *As a ratepayer I am very disturbed at the present unsatisfactory manner under which the Brigade now operates– if the various reports in the local press are correct*
>
> *Presumably there must have been some good reason for the Chief of the Brigade resigning after having been attached to the Brigade for twenty years.*
>
> *The Council being responsible for the Committee which accepted such a resignation without even taking the trouble to enquire into matters has failed in its duty to the ratepayers of the district whose interest and welfare it is its duty to study.*

At the present time it appears that there is only one man on duty at a time. I am informed that this man is also responsible for sounding the siren in the event of an air raid, and therefore must not leave his post and telephone under any circumstances.

As the Police Authorities have taken over the Fire siren for the purpose of raid warnings, may I ask how it is expected to call the Brigade in the event of Fire?

May I also remind the Council that there are I believe about 4,000 persons resident in Selsey district (which covers a large area) in addition to a considerable number of cripple children at a Holiday Camp.

Under these circumstances I should imagine the Home Office would have provided (if asked) at least one or two trailer pumps for which the Council should have organised a volunteer AFS crew.

Finally is it reasonable to employ one man and one relief working in twelve hour night and day shifts without making any arrangements to give them at least one day a week rest?

Many other residents are seriously perturbed at the present lack of an efficient Fire Service, to which they, as ratepayers, are entitled.

I am forwarding a copy of this letter to the Home Office for their information.

The very same evening there was a significant fire only a few hundred yards away from Mr Ralf, at 'Asphodel' in Beach Gardens, off Seal Road. The site of the fire still exists on the left hand side of Asphodel Cottage, 10 Beach Gardens.

All that remains of the house is the gatepost bearing its name

A report of 16th May 1940, in the 'West Sussex Gazette' indicates the scale of the fire:

> *A fire of such magnitude as Selsey has rarely, if ever, witnessed before, occurred on Saturday evening, at Asphodel, Seal Road, the home of Mr & Mrs Prescott. The fire started in the thatched roof and spread with great rapidity owing to the high wind, and the Fire Brigade had difficulty in preventing it from reaching the neighbouring bungalow where evacuees were housed. They worked for eighteen hours before it was safe; meanwhile the children and their belongings were accommodated in the chapel or in other houses. Many people assisted to save Mr & Mrs Prescott's furniture. In the heat of the moment one of the firemen seemed likely to lose his uniform, but the discomfiture was temporary, and all was well. No life was lost and no one was injured.*

The morning after the fire found Mr Ralfs penning a second letter to Selsey Parish Council:

> *re Selsey Fire Brigade*
>
> *With reference to my letter of the 11th inst, in which I enclosed a copy of my letter to the Chichester Rural District Council, I would refer you to the serious fire which occurred at Selsey yesterday (Saturday evening) which resulted in the destruction of a large detached house, from which you will see that my remarks were completely justified.*
>
> *If this fire had occurred late at night it is very probable that life would have been seriously endangered.*

Correspondence continued for some years covering the transfer of ownership. Finally, on 5th August 1941, A R Hayman, the Treasurer of Chichester Rural District Council, wrote to Mr Vince, Clerk to Selsey Parish Council:

> *Fire Brigades' Act 1938*
>
> *I have to refer to the above Act and to the property of the Selsey Fire Brigade taken over by the Rural District Council under Section 6 of the Act. It is regretted that pressure of work has prevented this matter being dealt with at an earlier date but as you are*

probably aware Section 6 (2) provides the Fire Authority shall pay to the Parish Authority such sum as may be agreed upon in respect of property taken over from the latter. I accordingly enclose a schedule of such property and equipment together with the value of each item.

The total of the valuation is £578.2.6. from which must be deducted outstanding Loan debt taken over by the Council on the 1st January 1939 amounting to £339.10.10. leaving a net amount due to the Parish Council of £238.11.8. This amount I am prepared to recommend shall be paid to the Parish Council in settlement of their claim. Before, however, submitting the matter to the appropriate committee of the Council I shall be glad if you will bring the matter before the Parish Council and obtain their views as to whether or not they are prepared to accept the amount of £238.11.8. In this connection I would draw your attention to the provisions of Section 2 of the Act which states, inter alia, that any capital sum so paid shall be treated as capital and applied with the consent of the Minister of Health and subject to any conditions which he may impose either in the payment of the debt or for any other purpose for which capital money may properly be applied.

A letter from the Clerk of the Parish Council dated 11th October 1943 stated:

The Parish Council have the sum of £238.11.8. on hand, being the amount received from the Chichester Rural District Council as the agreed value of the Parish Fire Engine on its transfer to the District Council. At a recent Parish Council Meeting it was resolved that an application be made to the Ministry to invest this sum in War Loan, and I should be obliged if the subject can receive consideration with a view to sanction being given to the proposal.

The Minutes of the next Parish Meeting record the acceptance of this proposition.

If nothing else, the history of the Selsey Fire Brigade teaches us that history does repeat itself. You may remember that in chapter 9 the Brigade became the laughing stock of the village because of its performance in Beach Road, owing to its badly maintained and quite inadequate equipment. Now at the end of this story, what do we find - a letter which once again highlights another case of inefficiency and suggested bad management. But this letter raises a more important issue, who should take responsibility?

The Chichester Rural District Council took over the management of the Fire Brigade but had forgotten about the administration and provision of an efficient Brigade and so, not unexpectedly, left the Parish Council to suffer the wrath of the community.

These circumstances are reminiscent of the incident that occurred in 1920 when the 'sacked' Fire Captain, Charles Wingham, suggested that he deserved at least a 'Putty Medal'. Is it the Chichester Rural District Council or the Selsey Parish Council that should be awarded such an accolade on this occasion?

16 – Selsey Fire Brigade Fire Captains

They had day jobs too!

We have gathered together the following information on the various fire captains of the Selsey Fire Brigade.

	START DATE	RESIGNATION DATE
Mr Alfred John Cutler	December 1909	22nd October 1912
Mr Augustus Charles Wingham	30th April 1913	13th October 1920
Mr William Edmund Hellyer	21st October 1920	9th January 1923
Mr William E Mitchell (Billy)	18th January 1927	4th November 1929
Mr Ralph Selsby	4th November 1929	November 1939

Alfred John Cutler

Alfred was born in the middle of the 19th century and little is known about his early life, but by the turn of the century he was a builder living in Selsey, in a property called St Elmo in New Road (now 33 Hillfield Road).

In August 1898, Alfred purchased a building plot (no. 11) from the Hundred of Manhood and Selsey Tramway Company. This plot was situated at the top end of Manor Road, almost opposite the site of the proposed hotel (The Selsey Hotel, which became the Stargazer and is now a block of flats) and cost him £77.10s.

Prior to his appointment as the Captain of Selsey's newly formed Fire Brigade at the end of 1909, Alfred had been the Captain of Chichester Fire Brigade. His experience was very useful to the Parish Council, who called upon his expertise to advise on equipment and continued to use his services as a builder and representative of the Water Company after he resigned in 1912.

Although he was a builder, he never got round to erecting a house on his Manor Road plot and, instead, sold it to Frank Stuart Potter for £60 in 1920. In 1923 Mr Potter did rather better and sold the plot for £100 to another builder, Jacob Berg, who built the house that is still there today (56 Manor Road). Fifty years on, in 1973, who was living there but the family of young Willie Lelliott – a former part-time fireman in the Selsey Fire Brigade!

Augustus Charles Wingham

Augustus Charles Wingham was born in 1873. Known as Charles, he became Selsey's second Fire Captain, in April 1913. As we have seen at the end of chapter 5, Mr Wingham was not altogether a popular Fire Captain and it is to him we owe part of the title of this book.

He was a blacksmith and wheelwright and also hired out pony traps (an upmarket version of the horse and cart). He lived in a thatched cottage called 'The Forge' on the east side of the High Street, across the road from West Street.

The Forge is the thatched building in the foreground

He and his wife, Alice Sophia had many children. Records exist of Elsie, Dorothy, Augustus Charles, Florence, Victor, Eric Ronald and Edith and there may be others!

Mr Wingham died in 1933, aged 60, followed the next year, sadly, by Augustus Charles junior, aged 31. Alice Wingham died in 1949, aged 78.

William Hellyer

William Hellyer was born in 1884. He started work in the 1890s with 'Darkie' Smith (Ron Smith's father) to whom he was an indentured apprentice. He served in WWI, in the Royal Engineers and, whilst serving in France, he was wounded in the shoulder with a lead shrapnel ball.

On 21st October 1920 William Hellyer became Fire Captain but he resigned after only two and a half years of service. Between the wars, he worked for the Selsey builders Bonnar & Bonnar, where he was the foreman for some years.

He was living at 'Glendelough' in Manor Road at the time he was appointed Captain, but by the beginning of WWII had moved to 1 Franklin Villas in East Street where he lived next door to his sister, Mabel Allen, who raised one of his daughters. He had a big moustache which, according to his granddaughter, Helen Homer, made her dislike kissing him. He was married and widowed three times, one of his wives dying two weeks after childbirth. He had two daughters – Rose who married Jack Norris and Pam who married Fred.

During WWII, Bill was 'directed labour' to Vosper's Boatyard at Portsmouth and used to travel daily from Selsey in Ron Arnell's car, for which he had a special petrol ration as their work was essential war work (it is thought they were building and outfitting MTBs and MGBs). After the war he worked for Ron Smith, the builder, with George Male.

He was a clever and gifted craftsman and is believed to have made the wooden staircase in 'Charges' – a Chichester shop on the site of the Midland Bank close to the Market Cross. This skill was confirmed by Brian Laurence, who now lives in New Zealand, who reports that 'Bill was a really first class carpenter and joiner and his knowledge of roofing, stairmaking and all aspects of the trade was really exceptional'.

He was still living in Selsey at 74 East Street in the 1950s, but when he eventually retired, in his 70s, he went to live with his daughter, Pam. He died in the early 1960s and is buried at Portfield Cemetery.

Brian Laurence's final comment was that 'Bill was a very fine man for whom I had the greatest respect.' A very fitting epitaph.

William Mitchell

Mr William Edwin Mitchell (Billy) was born in 1895 and came to Selsey in 1912 from his birthplace, Steyning, to work with Maidment's Garage, agents for cars and motor cycles. Between 1915 and 1919 he saw service with The Royal Army Service Corps, Transport Division, and rose to the rank of Company Sergeant Major.

Company Sergeant Major W E Mitchell

On 25th December 1919, at the United Methodist Church, Selsey, Billy married Ethel Mary Head, the second daughter of Stephen Head and Harriett Sarah Girdler, of High Street, Selsey. Mrs Head lived to the remarkable age of 102 years and was the owner of the controversial Myrtle Cottage almost until her death in 1972 (Myrtle Cottage was situated to the left of the Co-op entrance, until it was pulled down overnight in the late 1980s, and some folk may remember it as the doctor's surgery in the 1970s). Stephen Head was a carrier, operating from what is now the Co-op site. He was also a fisherman and lifeboatman.

William and Ethel went to America in 1922 ostensibly to settle with relatives in Salt Lake City, Utah, but they did not stay. Returning to Selsey, Billy started a business known as W E Mitchell, Builder, Selsey, which was responsible for the building of many fine houses in the village.

Billy Mitchell became Selsey's fourth Captain in January 1927, when he was instrumental in reforming the Selsey Fire Brigade, with Ralph Selsby. In the 1930s his brother, Edwin Lawrence Mitchell (Ted)[43] joined the brigade, together with brothers-in-law William Head and Fred Stephen Head. Billy was also a Special Constable and received a Long Service and Good Conduct Medal during the reign of King George V.

Billy Mitchell's workforce

He continued in the building business until his retirement in 1934 when he sold it to his brother-in-law, Fred Head, and Jim Smith and it became Head & Smith, Builders.

For two years following his retirement, William and Ethel travelled the globe on the

---

[43] Ted farmed Warner Farm at the very end of Warner Lane as well as a large piggery about 100 yards after the Gas Works. Roger Brand's Lawnmower Business now occupies part of this land.

RMS *Mataroa* and the *Reina del Pacifico*. They visited North, Central and South America, New Zealand and Fiji.

With the onset of WWII they were living in 'Ethwyn', in Ursula Square. William joined The Royal Observer Corps and was appointed Head Observer.

He was a member of the Selsey Masonic Lodge (now St Andrews Lodge) and was also a founder member of the 1st Sussex Principals Chapter 3672, a Cancer charity linked to the Masonic Lodge. Billy continued to live in Selsey, latterly in Lavender Cottage, Station Road, until his death in 1954. Ethel died in 1978. There were no children.

Ralph Selsby

Ralph's father came from Ashington and worked as a gardener at Beacon House, owned by Mr Woodman. Ralph himself was born in 1897 and, after leaving school, started work on Mr Wiggington's Park Farm, north of the village. He joined the Territorial Army (1st/4th Battalion, Sussex Regiment) and was discharged at Newhaven in 1914, aged 16, never having been to France. Ralph had been taught to drive by Mr Maidment and, when his brother joined up, Ralph took over his job as a chauffeur at St Kilda in Seal Road. He rejoined the Army in 1916, serving in the Transport Corps.

When he came out of the Army he bought a Ford lorry and started up in business as a carrier. He also had horses and worked with Rupert Gardener at the back of the Cinema. He left there and moved, firstly, to Warner's Yard, now part of Budgen's car park, and then to School Lane (where the Landerry industrial estate is now). Ralph also hauled huts for Mr Berg from Shoreham and Hilsea.

Ralph Selsby's horse & cart in the 1920s

He joined the Selsey Fire Brigade in about 1924 and became Captain on 4th November 1929, the 20th Anniversary of the Selsey Fire Brigade. A few years later he was instrumental in acquiring the Dennis fire engine after he saw it at a fire display at Shoreham and made enquiries.

The Selsbys lived in 'Ralda' in Lewis Road. The house is now called 'Little Prairie' and stands only 50 yards from where the fire appliance was kept, alongside Maidment's workshop.

At one time Ralph had a butcher's shop (where Seale Butchers is today) and he rented a farm across the road from the Lifeboat Inn (then called The Albion). This was Fish Shops Farm and he continued his tenancy until it was sold in 1963.

As we can see, Ralph Selsby was a man of many parts. He ran a haulage business from where Manhood Builders is today. By the gate, on the High Street, stood a timber shed which was the office where Mrs Selsby took the orders and did the bookwork. Much of the business was supplying such items as sand and ballast to local builders.

The Timber Shed in 1926

Phone 112

Pig and Poultry Farmers
New Laid Eggs
Moderate Charges
Personal Attention

HIGH STREET, SELSEY-ON-SEA

Mr Holden   Jan   1938

Dr. to R. SELSBY & Co.
(R. Selsby, W. E. Mitchell and E. L. Mitchell)

Coal Merchants and Contractors

Cesspits emptied by latest appliances

He bought 'The Quarry' (behind the police station, in Chichester Road) from Mr Thornton of Selsey Estates and during WWII hauled ballast for the Apuldram and Selsey advanced landing grounds.

As well as his other activities, he was a coal merchant and his billhead also advertised 'Cesspits emptied by latest appliances'. He owned the Malthouse brick field on the east side of the High Street, behind the present day British Legion, and employed Bill Mariner as his brickmaker. He was also a demolition man (he demolished Beacon House), a refuse collector, and a member of the Selsey football team.

Ralph Selsby with the Dennis Fire Engine

Mr Ralph Selsby saw the migration of the Selsey Fire Brigade from the control of the Selsey Parish Council to that of West Sussex County Council in 1939. He was obviously not keen on being under the control of WSCC as he resigned at the end of 1939, just as the transfer of power occurred, handing over the Captaincy to Mr Bert Sayers.

and Finally…

Plus ça change, plus c'est la même chose - The more things change, the more they are the same[44]

This is one man's account of more recent times and it shows that maybe things are not very different from 1909!

Ken Skeet and I were asked to join the Fire Service in the early 1960s to take the place of Cecil Stone and Edgar Terry. At that time I was working for Cecil at his yard in Church Road.

I had to wait a couple of weeks for the gear to come through. Finally, the Station Officer told me I could ride on the fire engine.

I was in the yard messing about. Oh! There goes the siren. After a few seconds - Blimey, that's me! Where's me bike?

I jump onto my bike and pedal furiously up Church Road. Don't bother about the traffic at Kingswells[45], straight round the corner, head down past the Legion (I didn't know it was this far. I wonder if I can make the crew? I was already puffing and panting). Straight up the High Street and into the Fire Station.

Off me bike. Sling it against the wall. Into the locker room. Where's me gear? Which is my peg? Number 6. Grab the gear complete with new shiny helmet.

I made it! Scramble on board. Albie's[46] the driver and already he's got the engine running. The Fire Chief, Jim Jerram, came in and told us we got a chimney fire on the council estate.

The Fire Engine pulls out into the main road. Four blokes on the back seat are trying to get dressed up, being shunted from one side of the vehicle to the other as the engine does 60 mph. Buster Keaton had nothing on us!

I try frantically to button up the tunic, all fingers and thumbs, putting the wrong buttons in the holes. Both legs go in the same hole of the leggings and my wellies are on the wrong feet! The adrenalin is going like mad.

---

[44] Alphonse Karr, *Les Guêpes*, 1849
[45] The corner of Church Road and the High Street
[46] Albie Mason – of blessed memory

It seemed as though Zonaker (Bill Arnell-Smith for the foreigners!) was always on the bell and, blow me, if he wasn't there again.

The engine tears back past the Legion, round the corner at Kingswells, down past the yard. (It didn't take half as long as me on my bike!) Then onto the council estate.

Everybody piles out of the engine. They grab the gear. Everybody seems to know what to do except me.

Ollie's[47] in charge of the rods and gets the sheet down to protect the floor. He sends me for a bucket of water. Zonaker's off in the roof to inspect the chimney inside to make sure there's no fire up there.

Gordon[48] tells me to put the stirrup pump in the bucket and start pumping. I do!

'Not Yet! Give us time to get the rods up the chimney, you blank blank!'

We carried on putting the rods up the chimney and I was pumping away until the fire was out. Once it was out and everybody was satisfied, we started clearing up, cleaning the gear and putting it back on the machine. The Fire Chief tells the people that they have to get the chimney swept before they light the fire up again.

Right-O, lads! Back to the Station! (Sounds like Trumpton, doesn't it?)

A more leisurely ride back. The adrenalin is easing down and things are getting back to normal. Pull into the station. Get told to wash down and clean the machine ready for the next shout. Clean me gear. Hang it back up on the peg. Sign the log book.

That's it. Me first shout! I'm in!

John Mariner

---

47 Ollie Kite
48 Gordon Ostle

Acknowledgements

The Selsey Society would like to thank the following individuals and organisations:

Colin Mitchell for pictures of and text about Billy Mitchell, photos of Ralph Selsby's business and an original photo of 'The Shack' fire.

Alan Readman of West Sussex Record Office for permission to use the photographs of the fire at The Pavilion and for organising the transfer of a portion of the film of The Shack onto a video for us.

Richard Childs of West Sussex Record Office for permission to use the photographs from Chichester Photographic Service Ltd.

West Sussex Record Office staff for their patience in assisting us to find fires.

Chichester Library staff for their patience in assisting us to find fires.

All Selsey Parish Council documents reproduced by kind permission of Selsey Town Council.

Chris Honywood for photos of the 'Heroes'.

Mollie Phillips for her donation of the Fire Brigade Committee Minute book.

Martyn West of the Chichester Museum for his documentation and information about the Dennis Fire Engine.

Dennis Ltd for permission to use their documents in our possession.

Surrey Record Office for their co-operation in providing documents.

Mr Dearsley for his permission to not only copy his film but also to use the portion showing the fire at 'The Shack'.

Ron Johnson for his advice about copyright on postcards.

Phil Bishop for the loan of his father's scrapbook and permission to use the pictures in it.

Kathleen Parsons for providing the picture of Mrs Sally Moore and herself and her sister Rita and for her permission to use it.

Madeleine Terry for lending us her family photos of the Fire Brigade.

Manhood Community College staff and students for organising the poster competition.

Selsey Library for hosting the Fire Brigade Exhibition.

Ron Hart for information about Ellis's Bakery.

May Swanson for her memories of the fire at Rookery Nook.

Tom Creedy and John Mariner for lending photographs and postcards.

Peter and Sally Rudman for preparing the draft chapters and subsequent proof reading.

Mike Hedges (late of Portsmouth Water) for his editing of the (nearly) final draft.

Hazel Ousley for her permission to use Clem Rose's photograph.

Richard Waterhouse of RPM Print & Design for providing us with the title of the book and for his dedication in making regular phone calls to ascertain our progress.

Andy Horner, District Commander, Chichester, West Sussex Fire Brigade for writing the foreword.

Hamptons International, Estate Agents, for supplying the picture of Coles Farm House and for allowing us to use it.

Helen Homer and Brian Laurence for their memories of William Hellyer.

Eddie Williamson for information about the Selsey Golf Club.

LAST BUT NOT LEAST, the Awards for All Organisation for awarding us the money to make the book possible.

Every effort has been made to trace the copyright holders and we apologise in advance for any unintentional omission. We would be pleased to insert the appropriate acknowledgement in any subsequent editions.

Newspaper reports, letters and minutes are quoted verbatim and therefore may include grammatical errors.

List of Fires

Date	Location	Page
19th Aug 1900	'Bathing Ranche' on corner of New Road (now Hillfield Road)	1
25th Aug 1909	Rick Fire at Common Farm (now North Common Farm)	4
30th Nov 1909	Hilton's Farm (Foot's Farm), corner of West Street and High Street	10
15th Dec 1911	The Shanty and Once Was, East Beach	17
4th Sep 1919	Two bungalows near the Marine Hotel, New Road (now Hillfield Road)	31
24th Mar 1924	Hay rick in East Road (now East Street)	44
24th Feb 1925	Frederick Forbes Glennie's new house, in a new road between the Selsey Tramway Station and East Beach (now Beach Road)	45
08th Oct 1925	Swiss Cottage, High Street	51
08th Mar 1926	Wilkins & Meades Stores, High Street	53
27th Jul 1926	Ellis's Bakery, High Street	54
21st Aug 1926	The Pavilion, High Street	55
31st Mar 1927	Fire at East Beach (no more details available)	64
05th Dec 1927	14 Station Road (now 22 Church Rd)	65
22nd Oct 1928	H J Hart and Sons, Station Road	67
31st Aug 1929	'Dawn', East Beach (now 97 Beach Road)	70
24th Oct 1930	Coles Farm, Norton	72

Date	Location	Page
22nd May 1932	7 Council Houses, (now 22 Beach Road)	76
17th Aug 1932	Rick Fire, Fish Shops Farm, near the Albion Hotel (now the Lifeboat Inn)	93
Nov 1933	Rick Fire, Fishshops Farm	109
28th Feb 1934	Club House, Selsey Golf Club	111
21st Aug 1934	'The Shack', Fishing Beach, Coastguards Lane	115
22nd Aug 1934	Store belonging to Mr Gray, carrier, close to Maidment's Garage and The Pavilion, off the High Street	117
Dec 1934/ Jan 1935	Pennicott's Drapery Store, High Street	121
30th May 1935	Motorcycle on old tramway bridge	123
19th Jan 1937	The Homestead, High Street	126
31st Jan 1937	Petersfield and Selsey Gas Offices, High Street	127
8th Aug 1937	Fun Palace, High Street	129
12th May 1938	Off Licence, High Street	130
14th Jul 1938	Fish Shop, East Road (now East Street)	133
18th Aug 1938	Orchard Avenue (no more details available)	134
11th May 1940	Asphodel, Beach Gardens, off Seal Road	142

INDEX

Albion Hotel/Inn	20, 21, 25, 93, 152	Boxall, PC	46
Albion Road	21, 25, 95, 110	Boyden, Reverend H A,	52, 53
Allen, Mabel	148	Bransby Williams, Mr	20, 56
Andrews, H	55	Brett, Superintendent (Chichester)	47, 55
Arnell, Ron	148	British Legion	153
Arnell, S B	83, 89, 90, 92, 101, 141	Bromley, Mr	29
Arnell, W E G	9, **13**, 30, 136	*Bryer*	57
Arnell-Smith, Bill (Zonaker)	156	Bucknill, Mr Justice	17
Asphodel	**142**, 143	Budden, J J Captain	4, 11, 29, 30, 31
Atlas Assurance Co. Ltd	131, 132, 133	Bunn Leisure	123
Auxiliary Fire Service	139	Bury, Mr	136
Ayling, John	95	*Byrerly*	25
Aylmore, Councillor	6, 11		
		Carver, Cyril	46
Bailey, F C	89	Charge, E	31, 32
Banff House	21, 25	Charges, Chichester	148
Barclays Bank	**iii**	'Casino Five' Band	138
Barford, Dr. P G	81, 83, 89, 90, 91	Cheffins or Chaffins, Mrs	17
Barnes, Fred (Coxswain Lifeboat)	115	Chichester Corporation Water Act 1897	6
Barnes, Mr	31	Chichester Fire Brigade	4, 6, 12, 30, 31, 45, 47, 50,
Barnesbury, London	119		52, 55, 57, 67, 73, 75, 93, 94
Barnett, PC	68	Chichester Observer	8, 10, 31, 50, 126
Baroona	21, 25	Chichester Police Court	46
Barrow, Mr	43	Chichester Post	45, 53, 67, 115, 117, 127, 137
Beach Gardens	142	Chichester Road	123, 153
Beach Road	45, 48, 76, 77, 79, 80, 85, 86, 144	Chichester Station	38, 42
Beacon Farm	93	Church Hall	56, 58, 83, 84, 85
Beacon House	151, 153	Church Road	44, 46, **65**, 79, 155
Beadle, Junior	94	Clarkson's Off Licence	127, **130**, 131, 132, 133
Bedford (Fire Engine)	103	Clayton Road	21, 22, 25
Belcham, Albert	70	Clayton, James	4
Benaton, J W L	54	Clayton, Luther	78
Benstead, Mr	29, 31	Clough, Len (or Les)	95, **104**, 109, 139
Berg, T Jacob	28, 43, 50, 78, 146	*Coastguard Houses*	21
Bill House	25	Coastguard Lane	20, 21, 25, 116, 117
Bilson/Billson, J	56, 57, 61	Coastguard Station	25
Bishop, A (Bert)	73, 95, **104**, 109, **118**	*Coffin's House*	21
Bland, RSM (London Scout Leader)	119	Coles Farm Nursery School	72
Bliss, PS	68	Coles Farm	**72**, 73
Bognor Fire Brigade	31	Common Farm	4
Bognor Observer	15, 17, 67, 73	Compton's Barn	20
Bognor Orchestral Society	61	Cooper, F B & Co	17
Bognor Regis Post	52, 57, 61, 74, 77, 80, 81, 85,	Cooper, Mr	18
	87, 89, 103	Corporation of Croydon	**41**
Bognor Urban District Council	31, 74	Cotlands Road	21, 25
Bonnar & Bonnar	148	*Council Cottages*	21
Bonnar Road	25	*Council Houses*	45, 76, 78
Botting, V	62, **64**, 66, 67, 69, 73	County Borough of Croydon	**37**, 39
Bottrill, Councillor	11	County Magistrates Chichester	95

Coxes Road	25	Fishing Beach	117
Croft Road	133	Fletcher, W H B	7
Cross Road	8	Fogden, W	11, 12, 30
Crossways	80	Foot's Farm	10
Crown Inn	16, 20, 21, 25, 55, 138	Ford Motors	87, 103
Cutler, W Alfred John	9, 12, 13, 19, 20, 22, 29, 30, 146	Forge, The	**147**
Cutts, A T	iii	Four Chestnuts, Chichester	5
		Francis, Mr	92, 123, 124, 136
Dabson PS (Chichester)	110, 120	Franklin Villas	148
Daily Mail	117	Fun Palace, The	**129**, 130
Danner Coastguard Street	21		
Dawn	**70**, 71, 72	Gardener, Rupert	151
Day, S H	81, 82, 83, 85, 86, 89, 90, 91, 101	Gardner, Mrs E	118
		Gardner, Mrs L	38, 48, 81, 83, 89, 123
'Delight' Concert Party	57, 58	Garland, Councillor	11
Den's Fish Bar	127	Garnier & Co	**24**
Dennis Bros Ltd/Engine	88, **97, 98, 99, 102,** 103, **104, 107,** 109, 110, **113**, 114, **118**, 120, **122**, 123, 124, 125, 137 152, **153**	Garrett, Mr	18
		Gimblett, G R G	iii
		Gladding, Son & Wing	60, 64, 73
Dewey, S	9, 22, **33**, 34, **37**, 44	*Glendelough*	35, 148
Downing, Mr	125	*Glengarrie*	25
Drapers and General Insurance Co. Ltd	121	Glennie, Frederick Forbes	45, 46, 48
		Godels	21, 25
Dunrobin	22, 26, 78	Grafton Road/Upper Grafton Road	21, 25
		Grasmere	79
East Beach Road	70	Gray, P (Carrier)	118, 119
East Beach	17, 22, 25, 26, 28, 44, 48, 64, 70, 71, 72, 96, 115	Gresford Colliery Disaster	137
		Groindene	49
East Road	16, 21, 25, 53, 109, 118, 119		
East Street	20, 53, 133, 148	Hales Farm	17
East Wittering Parish Council	104, 105, 106	Hamilton, Sir Archibald	136
Eastgate Square, Chichester	4, 6, 11	Hampshire Telegraph and Post	112, 115, 119
Elliott, Frank	2	*Happidais*	26
Ellis & Sons, Grocer	**54**	Harman, J,	95, **104**, 109, 132, 136, 139
Ellis, Ray	62, **64**, 69	Hart, H J & Messrs	21, 25, 43, 66, 67, 68, 69
Elsinore	56	Hayman, A R	143
Emlyn	21	Hazeldine, F J	28
Ethwyn	151	Head, Fred Stephen	95, **104**, 109, 139, 150
		Head, William	62, **64**, 66, 67, 69, 71, 73, 95, **104**, 109, **116**, 150
Faers, J	106		
Farlow, Vernon King	71	Head & Smith, Builders	150
Farrar, Gwen	59	Heaver, Mr	136, 137
Fidler, W	**38, 42**	Hellyer, William Edmund (Bill)	35, 146, 148
Fire Brigades' Act 1938	141	Hemmons H B	17, 18
Fire Brigade Widows & Orphans Benevolent Fund	136, 137	Hendry, James Ltd	**63**, 64
		Heron-Allen, Edward	85, 91, 92, 126, 127, 136
Fire Services Act 1941	139	High Street	15, 17, 21, 25, 42, 50, 51, 52, 53, 54, 55, 57, 75, 119, **121**, 126, 127, 128, 129, 130, 131, 132, 133, 147, 152, 153, 155
Fish Shop	133		
Fish Shops Farm	93, 94, 95, 109, **110**, 151		
Fisher, Mr	1, 2, 3	Hillfield Road	1, 21, 25, 31, 56, 71, 130, 146
Fisherman's Joy Inn	20, 21, 25	*Hillinglea/Hillingly*	21, 25

Hilton, Mrs	10	Leyland	103
Hilton's Farm	**10**, 11, 15	Lifeboat Inn	93, 152
Hobbs, Mr	137	Lighting and Watching Act 1833	14, 15
Hobden, Mrs A	57	*Little Prairie*	152
Hobden, W	61	Lloyds Bank	126
Holt, Alderman	8	Local Government Act 1894	1, 15
Holt, Second Fire Officer	4, 11	London & Lancashire Insurance Company	109
Homer, Helen	148	London & Westminster Properties Co.	89
Homer, Miss	57	London Fire Brigade	86
Homestead, The	**126**, 127	Lower East Street/Road	21, 25
Honywood, Christopher	136	Lummus, T F (Chichester)	49
Hooper, Captain (Chichester)	47, 52, 55, 67		
Hopkins, Fireman (Chichester)	4	MacDermott, Reverend	50
Hopkins, Walter F	75, 78, 80, 81, 82, 83, 85, 86, 87, 89, 90, 101	Maidment, Lewis (senior)	32, 33, 36, **38**, 41, 43, 44, 49, 50, 53, 56, 57, 60, 61, 62, 64, 65, 77, 80, 82, 85, 86, 87, **88**, **97**, 101, 102, 103, 106, 109, 117, 118, 119, 138
Horner, Andy	i		
Hughes, M T (WSCC)	**108**		
Humphrys, Dr	90, 91	Maidment, Lewis M (junior)	57, 61, 62, **64**, 66, 67, 73, 104, 109, 110, 118, 139
Hundred of Manhood Selsey Tramway Co.	146		
Hunnisett, Mr	136	Maidment, P W (Pert or Perk)	57, 61, 62, **64**, 66, 67, 69, 73, 95, **104**, 109, 139
Huntley, G P & Co	59		
		Maidment's Garage	115, 117, **118**, 119, 149
Ide, Mr	14	Male, George	148
Innerleithen	25	Male's Forge	21, 25
International Stores	53	Malthouse Brickfield	153
Itchenor Sailing Club	115	Manhood Builders	67, 152
		Manor, The	14
Jeavons, Gordon	79	Manor House Restaurant	79
Jenner, Thomas Wilson	65, 66	Manor Lane	48
Jerram, Jim	139, 155	Manor Road	21, 25, 35, 71, 77, 79, 80, 146, 148
Johnson, T Spencer (Spen)	62, **64**, 67, 69, 71, 73, 95, 104, 109, **116**, 137	Marine Hotel	2, 16, 20, 21, 23, 25, 31, 32
Jones, P	118	Mariner, William (Bill)	153
		Marks, Mr	136, 137
Keep, G F	91, 112, 124, 125	Marshall, B W	62, 64, 66, 67, 69, 73
Kennett, A	106	Mason, Albert (Albie)	155
Keys, Nelson	59	Mason, E (Ted)	94, **104**, 109, 113
Kingsway	116	Mayerl, Billy	59
Kingswells	155, 156	McGregor & Co	**38**
Kite, Ollie	156	MacNeille, Malcolm	116, 117
Klaxon Ltd	**48, 49**, 65	Meades Stores	**53**
		Meades, W	11
Lamb, Major R J	**63**, 89, 90	Meakin, R	32
Large Acres	127	Merryweather, Messrs	27, 36, 88, **100**, 103
Lavender Cottage	151	Mitchell, Edwin Lawrence (Ted)	**104**, 109, **116**, 150
Lee, J	95	Mitchell, J	20, 95
Legal Insurance Company	134	Mitchell, William E (Billy)	62, **64**, 66, 67, 72, 136, 137, 146, **149, 150**
Legg, Percy	11		
Lelliott, W (Bill)	51, 147	Moore, Henry, Sally, Ted, John, Kathleen, Rita	**76**, 77
Lewis Road	17, 21, 25, 118, 152		
Lewis, F Second Officer (Chichester)	47, 67	Moore, Lieutenant-Colonel W G	81, 83, 85, 87, 89, 138

Morris Motors	87, 103
Morris, PC & PS (Chichester)	53, 110, 120
Myrtle Cottage	149
National Fire Brigades' Association	**26**, 123, 132
National Fire Service	139
New Road	1, 20, 31, 56, 146
Newnham, John M	**39**
Nixon, A J	105, 106
Norris, Rose & Jack	148
North Common Farm	4, **5**
North Road	21, 25
Norton Lea	78, 112
Norton Main Road/Norton Corner	21, 72
Norton Priory	21, 26, 28
Norton	20, 21, 26, 73
Oakwood	33
Observer and West Sussex Recorder	1, 4, 55, 56, 60, 70, 93, 111, 120, 123
Off Licence House	42, 43
Once Was	17, 18,
Orchard Avenue	134
Osman, PC	53, 57, 67, 68, 95, 110
Ostle, Gordon	156
Ousley, Hazel (née Rose)	127, 128
Owens, Mr	32, 139
Page, William	95
Park Farm	151
Parker, Mr	33
The Pavilion/Selsey Hall	42, 53, **55**, 56, 57, **58, 59**, 60, 61, 65, 118, 136, 137, 138
Peacock, Mr	31
Pelham, Captain	1, 2, 3
Pennicott's Drapery Store	**121**, 122
Penny Lane	121
Pennycord, Mr	110
Petersfield & Selsey Gas Office	127, 128
Petts, Hilda	133
Phillips, Mollie & Frank	136, 139
Phipps, F W	42, 44, 55, 56, 57, 59, 60
Phoenix Assurance Company Ltd	54, 58, 69, 71, 133
Poor Law Amendment Act 1867	15
Pope, PC	23, 44, 46, 51
Potter, Frank Stuart	146
Pratt, R (Bob)	119, 139
Premier Riding School	118
Prestcott, Mr & Mrs	143
Prior, W	92
Quarry, The	153
Ralda	21, 152
Ralfs, Mr	141, 142, 143
Rasell, W D	24, 30
Rasford, Mr	32
Reeves, Mr	51
RNLI	117
Roman Catholic Church (site of St Wilfrid's)	67, 68
Rookery, The/Rookery Nook	45, **46**, 48
Rose, Tony (Hazel's brother)	127
Rose, Walter Clement (Clem)	127, **128**
Royal Exchange Assurance	128
Rudwick, Mr	139
Rusbridge, C	72, 73, 75
Rusbridge, Mr	48, 50
Salt Haven	71
Sargeant, Lawrie	79
Savage, PS	68
Sayers, Albert (Bert)	62, **64**, 66, 69, 71, 73, **104**, 109, 136, 139, 154
School Lane	8, 151
Seagar, J E	93
Seal Road	22, 142, 143, 151
Seale Butchers	152
Sell See Beds	53
Selsby, Ralph	44, 62, **64**, 67, 71, 72, 73, 74, 75, 76, 77, 78, 82, 83, 85, **88**, 89, 91, 95, 101, **104**, 109, 110, **116**, 118, 123, 127, 129, 136, 138, 139, 146, 150, **151, 152, 153**, 154
Selsey Estates	7, 93, 94, 95, 96, 153
Selsey Football Team	153
Selsey Golf Club/House	55, 58, 71, 111, **112**, 113
Selsey Hotel	21, 25, 32, 47, 79, 146
Selsey Nursing Association	138
Selsey Ratepayers Association	79, 83
Selsey Rectory	20
Selsey Society (Local History Group), The	136
Selsey Tramway & Station	**13**, 46, 48
Selsey War Memorial	45
Selsey Water Company/Works	7, 8, 12, 16, 19, 23, 27, 28, 44, 45, 83, 85, 90, 91, 138
Selsey Women's Institute	59
Selsey's Handcart in EWPC Livery	**105**
Selsey-on-Sea Ltd	6, 7, 95
Serena	22
Serjeant/Sargent, Dr of Hounslow	116, 117
Shack, The	115, **116**, 117
Shand Mason & Co.	10, 12, **13**, 36
Shanty, The	17

Sherriff, Mrs	71, 72
Sherrington, H J	31, 106
Sidlesham Mill	**47**
Simms, Messrs	106
Simonis (Fire Engine)	103
Skeet, Ken	155
Smith, Clifford E (Darkie)	55, 57, 60, 61, 148
Smith, H A	20, 44
Smith, Jim	150
Smith, Ron	81, 83, 89, 148
Somerleigh	21, 25
South of England Advertiser	112
St Albans	25
St Clement's Troop	119
St Elmo	146
St Kilda	151
Staffa	25
The Stargazer	79, 146
Station Hotel	8
Station Road	21, 25, 44, 46, **65**, 66, 67, 151
Stone, Cecil	155
Summers, Henderson & Co	117
Sun Insurance Office	72, 130
Suntop	141
Swindell, Mr	91, 127
Swindell, Mrs	127
Swiss Cottage	50, **51**, 52
Tate, Harry & Co	59
Taylor, Charles Seymour & Co	**89**
Terry, Edgar	155
Tetsworth House	21, 25
The Post	129
Thornton Heath Fire Station	37, 38, 39
Thornton, Mr	153
Titchenor, Mr	11
Town Police Clauses Act 1847	6
Tucker, H	62, 66, 69, 71
Turtle, Mr	**37**, 38, **49**
Twitchell, Right Reverend Bishop	56, 58
United Methodist Chapel	20, 21, 51, 149
Upfold, George	72
Upper Norton	78
Ursula Square	151
Village Green, Selsey	20
Vince, C E	25, 81, 82, **84**, 85, 89, 143
Vincent Road	21, 25
Vospers Boatyard	148
Wakely, Chas. M C	14, 15, 30, 31, 32
Walsh, Mrs	32
Wannop, & Falconer	73
Warner's Yard	151
Warren, Colonel	136
Warship Week	139
Welback	25
Welcome, Fireman (Chichester)	4
Weller, Third Officer (Chichester)	47
West Street	10, 16, 20, 21, 25, 71, 79, 130, 147
West Sussex County Council	92, 93, 101, 103, 106, **108**, 154
West Sussex Gazette	6, 7, 10, 55, 57, 68, 73, 95, 117, 120, 130, 143
Westhampnett RDC	7, 24, 26, 28, 29, 80
Westminster Fire Office	122, 128
White, W Llewellyn	89, 90, 92, 101
Wiggington, Mr	151
Wilkins, Butchers	**53**
Williams, G	62, **64**, 66, 67, 69, 71
Williams, H A	56
Willshire, W & Miss	51, 52
Windy Ridge	71
Wingham, Augustus Charles	20, 29, 30, 31, 33, **34**, 81, 89, 145, 146, 147
Wi-Wurry	22, 25
Woodman, Arthur H	16, 17
Wren, Percy	11
Wyatt, & Son	95, 96
Wyatts, Messrs	6
Wynshaven	25
York Road	141

Back Cover photo:

The New Dennis Fire Engine with Crew, 1933

Back row L to R: Bert Bishop, Bill Head, Ted Mitchell, J Harman, Les Clough
Front row L to R: Lewis Maidment, Bert Sayers, Perk Maidment, Ted Mason, Fred Head, Spen Johnson, Ralph Selsby